All I Thought Was True

K. A. Kottka

Fort Bragg
California

All I Thought Was True
Copyright © 1999 K. A. Kottka

All rights reserved. No portion of this book may be reproduced by any means, except brief excerpts in the context of review. For information, or to order additional copies, contact:

Lost Coast Press
155 Cypress Street
Fort Bragg, CA 95437

(707) 964-9520
fax: (707) 964-7531
email: lostcoast@cypresshouse.com

Author's photograph by Larry Strong

Epigraph from "In a Dark Time" by Theodore Roethke, Courtesy of Doubleday, A division of Random House, Inc.

ISBN 1-882897-31-5
Library of Congress Catalog Card No.: 99-71505

First edition

Printed in the U.S.A.

All I Thought Was True

*"What's madness but nobility of soul
at odds with circumstance?..."*

— Theodore Roethke

CHAPTER ONE

THE JOLT WHEN THE PLANE HIT THE TARMAC would have registered 3-plus on the Richter scale. Overhead luggage containers popped open, and oxygen masks first sprung free, then dangled like empty nooses.

Art, eyes wide, sweat flowing, pressed his face to the plane's window. Fear and adrenaline surged inside him; his heart pounded to the point he felt it would break through his chest. He tried to focus his sleep-filled eyes on the tarmac, now forty or fifty feet below because of the plane's bounce. Near panic, he strained to locate the missing sandbags, the artillery and machine gun positions.

The morning sun's first rays and the pilot's embarrassed laughter brought him back: "Sorry 'bout that landing, or near landing folks. We have plenty of empty runway, and this time I'll do it right," he promised.

In minutes, the plane neared its arrival gate. The stewardess' voice ended any remaining confusion: "Welcome to Will Rodgers International Airport in Oklahoma City. The captain asked me to apologize if he startled any of you. We'll be at our gate momentarily. Please remain seated with your seat belt buckled until we indicate it's time to deplane."

Outside the terminal, Art waited for his bus to Norman. A car exhaust's loud bang sent him to the ground. Muscles strained to force his body into the cement as he waited for the heat and debris to follow. When he felt and heard nothing, Art ventured a glance around and above him. People standing near him stared, motionless, some visibly shaken.

As he rose, knees wobbling, hands trembling, a police officer took his arm to help. "Are you all right Lieutenant?" he asked.

"I, I think so," Art responded, barely audible.

"My office is just a few feet from here. Care for a cup of Java?"

"Good idea."

Inside the small, warm office, the police officer poured two cups of coffee, "Do you take yours with anything?"

"Black's fine," Art answered with no intention of trying to raise the cup with his shaking hands, just glad to be free from public scrutiny.

"How long you been back in the States?"

"Five days. I processed out at Fort Ord. Sorry about the scene."

"Don't be. I got back eighteen months ago and still have problems. It'll take some time and understand, these people don't have a clue. I left Nam just in time to miss that Tet thing a year ago January. I heard it was really something."

Art nodded his assent. "I got there just in time to make it. Most everything was pretty tame after that."

"You from these parts?" the police officer asked.

"No, but I did my BA at OU. I'm going back to teach and finish my masters. I have a few months before the fall semester starts. Maybe I can settle down by then."

The police officer smiled warmly. "Just take it slow; try not to react. You'll need some time."

"Yeah, looks like," Art said as he stood to leave, "It's going to be different."

CHAPTER TWO

Two months later as Art walked across Oklahoma University's south oval, he had attained a level of inner peace. The time alone to think and write had helped settle him back into the land he'd left over three years before and had helped distance him from the chaos of Southeast Asia.

He felt secure on the familiar turf and silently thanked the late summer sun for being gentle to the grass and flowers. Their colors and aromas blended with an early September breeze to stir memories of crisp days and falling leaves in the Chicago of his childhood.

Everything here looked close to what he remembered. His destination, Stevens Hall, the new humanities building, was the only major change.

Even the students, many with long hair, headbands, beads, and bell bottoms, looked much like the young people with whom he had enrolled nine years before when he was a freshman.

A few coeds glanced curiously at him and his faded Army fatigue jacket. One turned her head and smiled directly at him as she passed. Art returned her smile but did not try to keep up with her brisk pace.

Inside Stevens Hall, he saw her veer into the room he sought. He guessed she'd made a wrong turn, but couldn't find her in the mass of people talking and laughing.

He sat near the top of the classroom, which was arranged in concentric circles, narrowing toward the podium and the distant lectern.

A man close to his age interrupted Art's search for the lost lady. "Hi, I'm Matt McGaw" the man offered, extending his hand. "Looks like a lot of new English teachers."

"Art Patowski," he responded, shaking Matt's hand. "They expect over four thousand freshmen; the baby boomer Sooners."

"Most of them guys looking for 2S deferments to stay out of Nam," Matt commented.

"From my biased but firsthand experience, I'd say good idea. But, Matt, what do you make of this room?"

"Looks new."

"I've never seen a classroom like this. It's more like med school than academia."

Matt did a complete turn in his chair, studying the room from every angle, even looking under the desk surface in front of him. He nodded approvingly. "The guy who designed this had his shit together. I'll bet twenty bucks with the right seating arrangements you can get beaver shots of every chick in class."

"Maybe this is where they teach future gynecologists," Art offered.

"Or recruit them," Matt added.

The noise lowered to a loud whisper as all seventy graduate students turned toward the back of the room.

In its far reaches by one of three doors, Dr. Carlton Pitts, their mentor for the next year, hovered above them. Large, red faced, arms full of miscellaneous paraphernalia, he swayed dangerously.

Peering down at them, he spied a golden-tressed damsel with prominent breasts. His wire-framed spectacles became telescopes focusing on his prey. Never taking his eyes off her, he placed his belongings on the nearest desk and navigated the five rows between them.

He stopped directly in front of her. "Helen," he roared, "thy beauty is to me like those Nicaen barks of yore that gently o'er the perfumed sea the weary wanderer bore to his own native shore, to the glory that was Greece and the grandeur that was Rome!"

Uneasy laughter rose at Pitts's corruption of the poem. He did not hear it. He took the young lady's right hand and planted a drool-filled kiss. Her confusion changed to revulsion. She pulled her hand away from the good doctor and frantically searched her purse for a handkerchief.

Pitts turned, grinning blindly, oblivious to her disgust. "Who wrote that?" he barked. When no student ventured an answer he laughed and challenged them with, "Who is the author?" as he climbed down to the lectern, waving his arms as though conducting a symphony, the odor of Irish whiskey exuding from every pore in his body.

"Ovid," "Swinburne," "the Marquis de Sade," "Jacqueline Susann," the audience called.

"No! No!" Pitts bellowed. "You call yourselves graduate students and can't identify one of America's foremost poets!" The hint of a smile betrayed his ostensible scorn. "Come now, let's see your mettle!"

A tentative voice near the podium rose above the din: "Professor, I believe it was Edgar Allan Poe."

Pitts squinted his bloodshot eyes, trying to discern the purveyor of this information. The answer had destroyed his playful mood. Unsuccessful, he attempted to focus on the rest of his audience. With no better luck, he fumbled around the lectern looking for the items left at the top of the room.

Frustrated, he stopped and again tried to find the student who'd answered the question. The eager would-be scholar grinned broadly and half-raised, half-waved his hand for the expected acknowledgment. Pitts's worn eyes discerned this movement. Those near the podium heard him mumble, "Another new asshole," only somewhat under his breath.

"Let's see how many new English teachers made it to orientation. Somewhere I have a roll sheet, but it's with my papers, which I seem to have lost." He staggered around the podium searching for the misplaced items. "Did I have anything when I came in?" he asked no one in particular.

"Here they are," a feminine voice offered. The students turned as the young woman who'd smiled at Art descended the stairs, Pitts's papers in hand.

"Thank you my dear," he said. "What's your name?" He managed to stroke both her arms in the exchange of papers.

"Melanie Slatter," she replied, darting back up the stairs.

She looked no older than seventeen or eighteen. Less than five feet tall, eighty-five or ninety pounds, with blazing red hair, her blue eyes, turned from Pitts, combined innocence with sensuality. Art saw their humor and intelligence. The form and flow of her body were a woman's.

After a moment, snapped back to consciousness, Pitts extracted mangled sheets of paper from his material.

"I'll pass the roll around and ask each of you to initial after your name. If you're not listed, print your name on the bottom of the sheet. Let me warn the comedians," he threatened, "John Milton, Margaret Mitchell, Shakespeare, Dante, have all enrolled here before. If I find their names on my roll sheet, I'll track you down by your handwriting. Sooner or later you'll take my course, and I'll get you!" He walked from behind the lectern, glared at the audience, and paced back and forth, attempting to appear menacing.

After a few seconds, he softened his stance and told them about life as graduate teaching assistants, dwelling on its pleasures and pitfalls.

"As you know or will soon learn, teaching is a joy. But do not," he warned, "fall in love with this oasis of cultural endeavor, as I did with my graduate school, and as all graduate students in all recorded history have. You are here as students to learn and as instructors to teach. Ultimately, you must leave, irrespective of your infatuation with this place!"

He paused on this supposedly dramatic statement, attempting to emphasize his point.

"Each of you must take the graduate qualifying examination. There are three possible grades: Ph.D. qualified, MA qualified and failed. You may take the exam twice. You will not be awarded any graduate degree until you've passed at the appropriate level. Are there any questions on this?"

There were none. Each student knew about the infamous test.

"One particularly difficult item," he continued, "concerns interactions with your students. Remember, always, you are their teachers, not their mothers, their fathers or, God forbid, their paramours! We've had several incidents and alleged incidents the last few years that have caused much difficulty. For God's sake, they're still children, even with their firm, young developed bodies, their vitality, their incredible skin tone and texture! Even though it's 1969, the Age of Aquarius, whatever the hell that means, remember your duty: To teach!"

Without raising his hand, Matt yelled out, "What if one comes on to you really strong?" Most of the students turned toward Matt, displaying the same mix of humor and confusion they had with Pitts.

Pitts waited a moment, as though deep in thought. "If it happens, send the student to me."

"I don't think he means the boys," Art whispered to Matt.

Two hours later, the meeting adjourned. When Melanie dashed out of the room, Art considered going after her but decided to wait for a more private time.

He led Matt to a pub called the Organ Grinder, a Norman watering hole with live entertainment. On the way, he explained to Matt that he'd taken his BA at OU and had completed a year on his MA before joining the Army. Art learned that Matt and his wife, Virginia, had been married less than a year and that despite her doubts, had left their Colorado home so he could pursue his doctorate at OU.

Inside the bar, two young ladies in bikini-type costumes wiggled around a small stage to juke box music. Intensely interested, Matt applauded their efforts.

"Now that's what I call talent. Look at those headlights on the blond. Man, I'd love to see 'em on high beam!"

They found a vacant table and ordered beers. "When you told me you did your undergrad work here, I figured you'd know all the local dives. Entertainment like that will make up for the 3.2 piss we have to drink."

"I've lived here seven of the last ten years and still don't like it," Art responded.

"How long before it affects me like real beer?" Matt asked, concerned.

"Two months and you'll get shit-faced like the locals."

"By then I'll be broke and have hocked my car and sold my wife into white slavery. I couldn't believe it when I ordered a martini downtown and they told me liquor by the drink is illegal."

"I know. My home's Chicago, where the bars never close. I wound up here via the Air Force. At 15 I forged a birth certificate and joined; I spent my last two year at Tinker Airbase, just northeast of here. After my discharge, I stayed and took my BA from OU. Later I joined the Army."

"You're a glutton for punishment," Matt commented, shaking his head. "Two tours with Uncle Sam and two here."

Art laughed. "There were circumstances."

"I couldn't take this place that long."

"Colorado is beautiful country," Art acknowledged. "I've been there a few times and loved it."

"I can finish the MA next spring," Matt explained, "and take a break for a year, then come back to finish the Ph.D. Maybe teach or work at a newspaper in ski country for the year I'm away."

"Sounds like a plan. What'd you think of the group?"

"Our new colleagues?" Matt shrugged his shoulders. "I'd say typical. Your average share of dorks, book-heads, creeps, recent grads who think the world can be saved by literature, and a few normal people like you and me, and I'm not too sure about you."

"What a cynic!"

"No, a realist. After six months most of those babies will have hair down to their asses, be wearing headbands and screaming about the war. All of which is fine, but it won't be because they know or understand anything. It will be because it's the thing to do. Then after they get their Ph.D.s, they'll cut their hair, burn their headbands, buy new suits and settle into academia, always reminding everyone what rebels they were and how they changed the world. It's more horseshit."

"Don't be too hard on them. I spent 15 months in Nam. The war stinks," Art responded quietly.

"When you say that I believe it because you've been there. I don't like the war either, but I'm not going to tell anyone he should or shouldn't go."

"Matt, I think you're after intellectual honesty," Art said, raising his bottle of Lone Star.

"No, actually, I'm after pussy, some like that on stage." They tapped their bottles together. "You might say I'm a man following my own heart-on." They drank and laughed.

"What's your grand design?" Matt asked.

"Supporting myself with the GI Bill and teaching will feed body and soul. The Government helped fuck-up part of my psychological support structure, so it can furnish a small piece of change while I reconstruct it."

"Don't forget the coeds." Matt added.

"I don't intend to."

That night, Matt helped Art back to his room in Newman Hall, a boarding house run by a Catholic church in Norman. In the months to come, Art would reciprocate the favor many times.

CHAPTER THREE

THE GODS WERE GOOD. Graduate students without master degrees shared offices with other less knowledgeable and worthy beings. Art, scheduled to complete his MA after the current semester, officed in a bullpen of eight graduate students, including Melanie Slatter.

Though pleasant, she rebuffed his entreaties to join him for a brew after a hard day of sentence fragments and comma splices. Art learned she'd been dating a Brit working on his Ph.D. in Philosophy, but he'd disappeared after the first days of the semester. She continued to give her smile to Art, which she didn't share with everyone, but he seemed unable to strike the right chord. Yet, Art felt certain they'd connect. He felt the electricity.

He just hoped it would be soon. While the time alone helped in sorting through the zany chaos of his recent past, the warmth and intimacy a relationship offered could facilitate his rejuvenation. He hoped he had something to offer in return, but could not see much beyond his own needs.

Teaching helped sublimate much of his excess energy. After the initial terror, he enjoyed the challenge despite on-going frustrations. Borrowing from teachers he thought effective, Art used the Socratic method in the classroom and encouraged the exchange of ideas through dialogue, but he learned that finding points of reference with which the students identified was difficult. He tried to involve them in discussions on topics he thought would interest them, but discovered the years separating them created a chasm.

"Look," he started in an early discussion on figurative language, "in the song 'Mrs. Robinson,' Simon and Garfunkel use the line, 'Where have you gone Joe DiMaggio, a nation turns its lonely eyes to you,' to express a feeling that something's missing from America. What is it?"

Art heard only the sound of silence.

"Okay," he asked, "what does Joe DiMaggio represent in the American consciousness?"

A few students shuffled uneasily in their seats.

"Let's talk about DiMaggio. Can anyone tell me about him?"

A student in an ROTC uniform half-raised his hand. "Wasn't he a baseball player or something?"

"How many of you know who DiMaggio is? Have you ever heard of him?"

The same student raised his hand.

Art felt old and tired. "How many of you know the song 'Mrs. Robinson?'" he asked.

All the students raised their hands.

Puzzled at their ability to accept the lyrics without any understanding, he decided to talk about DiMaggio. Art sat on the front of his desk and took a moment to envision the great ball player he'd seen roaming Comiskey Park's center field.

"DiMaggio played for the New York Yankees baseball team in the late thirties and in the non-war years of the forties. His performance took on epic proportions. He became a living legend. Joe did it all. When he ran, he glided like a gazelle. He hit with power and in the clutch. Whatever the Yankees needed to win, DiMaggio delivered, and he delivered with class. He didn't say much. He let his performance on the field talk for him. I think Simon and Garfunkel are saying America needs the heroic leadership DiMaggio symbolizes, but 'Jolting Joe', and men like him, have 'left and gone away.' There's no one to take his place, but we need heroes for all kinds of reasons. So what can we do? What does Mrs. Robinson do?"

The class stared at him, distant and silent.

One student finally raised a hand.

"Yes?" Art asked full of hope.

"As I recall," the student began, "she screwed Dustin Hoffman. But it's been over a year since I saw the movie."

Art took a moment to respond. "Let's forget the movie and think about the song."

A few students tried to appear as though they were thinking. This took the form of various pained expressions.

Art surrendered. "We'll pick this up in the next session. Any questions before we go?"

A student raised his hand. "Was DiMaggio as good as Mickey Mantle?"

"They were different types of ball players," Art responded, "from their lifestyles to the way they played the game. But I wouldn't hesitate a second in taking DiMaggio, if I had to choose between them."

"Didn't Mantle replace DiMaggio?" the same student asked.

"Yes," Art answered, "Mantle did. Perhaps that's part of Mrs. Robinson's problem. Perhaps that says it all."

Besides teaching, Art had enrolled in three classes, the last nine hours for his MA. The Poe, Whitman, and Dickinson class met late in the afternoon on Monday, Wednesday and Friday. He enjoyed the material, but not the professor, Horace Manly.

A troubled soul, Manly had dedicated his life to the study of Nathaniel Hawthorne and had embraced the author's bleak vision concerning the human condition. Manly's brooding countenance and palpable despair combined to make him popular with a faction of graduate students who clung to a precipice over the slough of existential despair.

Tall and thin with a nose that reminded Art of Ichabod Crane, Manly went to various graduate student parties, especially those hosted by his admirers. Early in the semester, Art and Matt were invited to a few of these shin-digs.

Manly always arrived with his pipe, his wife and his intellectual baggage. With no other faculty members present, he pontificated and spread the vision of his dark gospel.

After their first meeting with Manly at one of these parties, Art and Matt debated the source of Manly's foreboding, concluding that his wife, pipe or vision had to be responsible.

"That lady makes Yassir Arafat look good," Matt stated. "She's the only woman East of Suez with a beak bigger than Manly's. If he'd replace his Price Albert with some choice pot and snuggle up with one of his groupies, Manly's world view would lighten considerably."

Art disagreed. "He's always miserable because he believes no matter what man does, he's conceived in sin, and part of him, no matter what his experience or how he grows, is damned. It's Hawthorne's view of humanity. The guy really buys it."

"No," Matt insisted. "There's nothing wrong with him that can't be cured by fine weed and a piece of ass. Not necessarily in that order."

In one Friday afternoon class, Manly had been particularly brutal to Poe, dismissing his work as superficial and calling him, "...at best an enigma, at worst, a perfect example of the neuroses underlying most American literature."

After class, Keith Drumright, a first year graduate student, joined Art on his way to the graduate assistants' office, and asked him how he liked the lecture.

"Manly went a bit overboard. If every guy who drank too much, wrote about ghosts and married his thirteen-year-old cousin were crazy, what would happen to rock n' roll?"

"Poe's tough to figure out," Keith stated. "He's an enigma."

"Give me a break!" Art did not want this conversation. As usual on Friday afternoon, except for them, the office was vacant.

"It's bad enough Manly laughs every time he mentions Whitman and can't get close to Dickinson, but I would have guessed Poe is right in tune with his thinking: a kind of Hawthorne on acid."

"Forget Manly and tell me about Poe," Keith insisted.

"If you're quoting Manly, we can't leave him out. You're telling me his thoughts, not yours. Poe didn't play games. He meant what he wrote, just like Manly's favorite fun-filled guy, Hawthorne. But Poe approached it differently."

"Did he achieve literature or pulp?"

At that moment Melanie Slatter walked into the office, freshman papers to be graded under her arms. She smiled, making eye contact only with Art.

"Excuse me," she said as she passed between them. She sat at one of the desks and proceeded to sort through the papers.

"Keith," Art responded, now even more anxious to end the conversation, "to discuss aesthetics, we all have to decide what and why we think literature is. But don't take Manly too seriously until you've read his aesthetic position."

"Read it?"

"Checkout his book, *Hawthorne's Perpetual Pessimism*. It explains his aesthetic, but I think it's muddled. What's more, I wouldn't pay too much attention to his opinions on Poe, Whitman, or Dickinson." Art glanced at Melanie. From what he could discern, she paid no attention to the discussion.

"You can't write him off so easily," Keith continued. "He's written a book, published articles, and he grades the Masters and general Ph.D. exams!"

"Fine, know what he wrote and thinks, but make your own determination as to whether he's right or wrong. That's all I'm saying."

"It's more complicated than that," Keith insisted. "You have to look at the political realities."

Art began to worry that this conversation would never end. He looked at Melanie. "What do you think?" he asked.

She looked up from her grading and met his eyes. "Fuck 'em if they can't take a joke!"

Art laughed. Keith stared glumly.

"An excellent point on which to end this conversation. I have papers to grade too. Let's work together," he suggested.

"Why not?"

He didn't believe his ears. "Keith, we'll pick this up later."

Dejected, the young man shrugged his shoulders and lumbered out of the room.

Art sat across the desk from Melanie. He waited until he heard the outside door to the building close.

"You're an angel of mercy. Having to put up with Manly on Friday afternoon is bad enough. But then to go on…"

"Keith knows you've completed a year of grad school and did a tour in Vietnam. He looks up to you. He thinks you're a man of the world," she interrupted.

"What am I to you?"

"Someone to grade papers with."

"Is that all?"

"I don't know you."

"Not my fault," he responded. "And not altogether true. We've been around each other for a few weeks, heard a few opinions."

She smiled that smile he loved. "I've heard some of your opinions. I doubt you've heard any of mine."

"You haven't said much, but it's not that I haven't tried."

"Maybe it's time we learned something about each other," she responded, emphasizing the word "each" and placing a hand on his.

Amazed at this sudden turn, he smiled and looked deep into her eyes. "Your eyes are beautiful."

She cocked her head to one side. "Not very original."

"Not meant to be. Just an honest statement about your eyes."

They remained silent for a moment.

"Tell me about you," he asked. "Where's your home, what do you like to do, what's important to you?"

"I'm from Missouri. I love games and sexy underwear."

"Games and sexy underwear?" he asked intrigued. "Two of my favorites. What kind of games?"

Melanie looked away in playful thought. "Pool and pinball machines. Bowling and miniature golf are okay."

"Are you good at pool?" He loved the game. On the south side of Chicago, it held religious status.

"I'm okay, but great at pinball. The best machines in Norman are at Orin's pizzeria."

"They're the only pinball machines in Norman," he responded.

"That's why they're the best."

"Let's start at the Library Bar with some beer and pool," he suggested. "Then we can go to Orin's for a pizza, more beer and pinball."

"Sounds good."

"Now, about the underwear..." Art asked raising one eyebrow.

"I spend all my discretionary money on games and sexy underwear."

"Why underwear?"

"It makes me feel good. You said you liked it too."

"Yes," he replied, "but I have to see it to decide. Which reminds me, Missouri's called the Show-Me-State. Ever model?"

"Sometimes. It depends on the circumstances."

"Your modeling underwear might be the prelude to the finale of a great evening."

"Maybe, but let's keep our priorities straight. Pool or pinball comes first."

He thought his happiness could resurrect the sinking autumn sun, or at least delay its decline. They put their freshman papers away and left for another of Art's old haunts.

The Library Bar had been called many different names and had known many owners. Little more than a rundown shack, it had at one time been a redneck hangout, and then a frat dive, but it was now a long-hair hangout.

Art preferred it to the cowboy bars, which reminded him of third world countries, and to the frat bars, which were too sterile for his taste.

In the Library Bar, Art could watch different life-styles mix in a live-let-live atmosphere, breached on occasion by a redneck who wandered in, or by a bad acid trip, or by too many swigs from a brown paper bag. But these were exceptions. A mellow atmosphere usually reigned.

They found a booth close to the pool table and waited for it to clear.

"How's the teaching going?" he asked.

"It's fun. The first day I sat down as though I were a student. I asked the guy next to me if he knew anything about the teacher. He said 'No, but he'd bet we'd get one of those jerk graduate students.' When I got up and introduced myself, you should've seen the look on his face."

Art laughed. "Did he stay in class?"

"Sure, why not? I didn't intimidate him."

"You could pass for an undergrad. At orientation, I thought you'd gone into the wrong room."

"Looking young isn't fun. You saw them card me," she said, indicating her beer. He raised his glass. "May they still be carding you twenty years from today. Then it will be fun."

"How are your classes going?" she asked.

"It's a mixed bag. Sometimes I'm able to get them enthused. More often, I feel as though I'm speaking a foreign language. When I grade their papers, I think they're the foreigners."

"Part of it," she responded, "is age and experience. Most of them have never been more than fifty miles from their hometowns, which aren't centers of urban sophistication."

"Hey, I understand. Though I grew up in Chicago, I learned little about anything but survival. I didn't know the difference between don't and doesn't until I failed Freshman English here."

"At OU?"

"I did. The prof now teaches next to me, shudders every time she sees me."

"That's wild. Tell me about Chicago and how you ended up here."

"I grew up on the south side in a lower, middle class neighborhood. At best, we worried about making three bucks an hour, at worst about staying out of jail. Poe, Whitman and Dickinson weren't hot topics. At fifteen, I got thrown out of high school for fighting. The love of my life learned I was too young for her and dumped me. I beat up the guy who told her my age, put him in the hospital. It sounds stupid now. Then, it meant everything. Things were bad at home. I altered a birth certificate and joined the Air Force. At some point, I started to think about college. Since I hadn't finished high school, it looked impossible. But I made it."

"You've come a long way."

"I don't know. Vietnam seems like a giant step backward, and wherever I am, I still have a long distance to travel."

After they got the pool table, Art won each game quickly and easily. Melanie, frustrated, suggested they find the pinball machines. He agreed. "If you're not better at pinball, I'm going to be concerned."

"Hey," she objected, "I wasn't ready for a pro. You guys from Chicago are all hustlers," she added with fake indignation.

"An English teacher shouldn't stereotype. There are many guys from Chicago who can't shoot pool. There are many guys from Oklahoma who can. Unfortunately, I've met most of them and bought them many rounds of brew."

"At Williams, I beat most of the girls."

"What do girls going to Williams know about shooting pool, and what the hell is a Williams grad doing here?"

"Look who's stereotyping now," she responded. He laughed. "You got me, but why are you here?"

"I graduated last December, spent the next six months in England, met a guy from London who goes to OU, and came here. I've been in Norman since June."

"Are you living with him?"

"We tried. It didn't work. He's in London now, should be back in the next couple of weeks."

"Is he your regular pool partner?"

"I don't have one. You can apply for the position, if you'll teach me how to beat you."

"It's a game of angles, finesse, concentration, practice...."

"Sounds like many things, life, love..." she said looking past him.

"It is. I don't know how far I'd take the analogy, but sometimes I think about becoming the best pool player in the world, Chicago Fats. But what's the point?"

"To be the best," she countered. "That's what most people want if they care about what they're doing."

"If pool's the number one activity in someone's life, something's wrong."

"But being the best at anything has to be terrific fun."

"You're probably right. At times, I've been there. Maybe just in a bar, but it's fun, just never enough. It looks like it would be when you see Joe Namath win the Super Bowl, see Mays hit a home run in the Series, but it never is."

"Until you've accomplished something on that level, can you be sure?"

"Good point," he conceded. "But Truth and Beauty can be accomplished only to a finite, repeatable point with great eye-hand coordination, whether it's pool or baseball, two activities I love. Now poetry, drama, they have possibilities."

"You're searching for Truth and Beauty?"

"Maybe."

"Do you write?"

"I started a play overseas. It's about a young soldier in Vietnam. I'm almost finished."

"Kind of a *Red Badge of Courage*? she asked.

"More of a *Siddhartha*. There's a lot of the physical in it, but it's part of his journey to a higher level of consciousness, to a general understanding of existence that transcends what any of us normally experience."

"Your journey?"

"I hope so."

She smiled at him. "Beauty is truth, truth beauty."

"Maybe that's why Keats died young. He'd found the answer."

"We've lost track of our priorities. We're back where you and Keith were in the office. I don't know if there's any hope for you."

"If I discuss these things with someone who is intelligent and knows something, I tend to get carried away."

"What's wrong with Keith?"

"It's looking up a dead man's ass. Keith has no opinions of his own. He repeats everything Manly puts on his plate with no critical analysis."

"What do you think graduate school is all about? You're here to become a scholar."

"That's their program, not mine. I want to finish the MA and my play, learn more about me. But whatever the direction is, I can't see myself, ever, regurgitating lamebrain ideas to wanna-be scholars. Life's too short. What about you?"

She took his hand. "I'll tell you later. There's a time and place for everything. Right now, our goals are to drink and play games. No more serious conversation."

"I'll try to curb certain propensities. Let's go to Orin's for pinball and pizza."

After midnight, they went to Melanie's apartment. She poured wine and played the Beatles' *Sergeant Pepper*.

His ignorance of Beatles' music amazed her, but Art explained that in school he'd worked forty hours a week and carried a full academic load, not leaving much time for pop culture. In Vietnam, the Officers Clubs presented an occasional rendition of "Yesterday" by Filipino or Thai entertainers, who did little for the Beatles' or any other Western music.

"I'll teach you all there is to know about the Beatles," she promised.

"It's the greatest pop music ever, and the best thing to come from Britain since the Bard."

Her British friend, Richard, flashed across his mind.

She lit a joint and poured more wine for them. Art quickly felt more relaxed than he had in years.

"I'm glad you're okay about the dope," she said.

He took the joint, unable to rid his face of a silly grin. "I'm a fan, if handled in moderation. I'd rather be around stoned people than people who've put away a batch of martinis. My only problem with grass is this stupid grin I can't get rid of." He leaned towards her to display his problem. She fell back into the sofa laughing.

"Why are you so far away?" he asked, slurring his words. "I'd love for you to sit close to me."

When she sat beside him, he put his arm round her and kissed her forehead. Her small frame reminded him of the Vietnamese women he'd known.

They giggled about many things, Pitts, Manly, the music, whatever they said, whatever they thought. She blew smoke into his mouth, the room started to spin. This seemed funny too. She poured more wine, then excused herself. In minutes she emerged from her bedroom wearing only sheer pink bikini panties and a matching bra. The living room became a make-believe runway for her modeling.

"I got this job because of my long legs," she joked.

He applauded. "They look good to me," he stated sincerely. Proportioned perfectly, her small firm breasts tilted upwards, in harmony with the curvature of her waist and hips.

Walking back and forth, she whirled around, stumbled into a table and knocked over a lamp. "Oops!" she laughed. "This wasn't here during rehearsal. I'll fire the stage manager!" She picked up the lamp, then looked at him. "What do you think?"

His eyes took her from head to toes, then back. "Fantastic," he responded, softly. He tried to stand.

"No, not yet!" she cautioned, turning and running back to her bedroom. She returned wearing a red teddy. He encouraged her to stop and sit with him. She laughed and ran to her bedroom, appearing quickly in another outfit.

She noted his obvious excitement. "That's better than an applause meter." He again started to stand. "Wait, one more!" she called, running back to the bedroom.

Art plopped back down on the sofa, feeling some frustration. "Just a sec," she called. He took a long drink of wine.

She reappeared wearing a black garter belt, black hose, black crotchless panties and matching bra. He sat stunned, a fantasy alive before him. His penis strained for open air and immediate suffocation. She knelt in front of him, and they kissed with mouths open, exploring each other slowly, thoroughly. He tried gently to pull her alongside him, but she resisted.

She undid his trousers and lowered them and his underwear over his steely hard-on, then threw his clothes across the room and began kissing him from his feet, working upward. When she reached his member, she licked away early liquid and ran her mouth over its head and down the shaft. He groaned in delight, the pleasure intense to the point of pain. She continued till convinced he'd reached full erection, then straddled him, squatting down hard to assure full penetration. Her wetness moistened the inside of his thighs.

He unhooked her bra and pulled her to him, alternately sucking each breast fully, slowly disengaging until he reached the nipple, which he clung to gently with his teeth before letting go.

With her eyes closed, head thrown back, he watched as she entered her own domain, thrusting up, down and around on top of him. She positioned him the way she wanted to experience it. Art felt that most of his body had ceased to exist, that he'd become a disembodied cock from which she took her pleasure. This new experience interested him and helped him maintain control. He lay back enjoying the sensations and watching her delight.

As her tension grew, her muted groans became louder. He started to pull her down and under him, but again she resisted. In a voice that made him think he might need an exorcist, she growled. "No! No! Stay there!"

Her appetite and intensity excited him as much as the physical pleasure.

After her third orgasm, he had to use every method he knew to contain himself. "Mays' great catch was in the '54 World Series, Vic Wertz the batter. Shakespeare wrote thirty-seven plays and one hundred fifty-four sonnets." No use. Willie and Will couldn't help him. His roar of release reached back to some ancient ancestor who scuttled across the floors of silent seas. He grabbed her bottom with both hands and raised his mouth to her breasts as he exploded inside of her.

When he stopped groaning and regained some level of awareness, he couldn't move. "Great!" he gasped. Still on top of him, she smiled, dismounted and curled into his arms.

They said nothing until he sat up and took a sip of wine and offered the glass to her. "No, thank you," she replied. "You really have intense orgasms."

"One a year has that effect. But what about you? With that first one, I'm surprised your neighbors haven't called the cops."

"It had been a while."

"Did you enjoy?" he asked expectantly.

"A good beginning, worth another try."

"Good beginning?" He looked at her in disbelief.

"Sex is somewhat like pool, you have to scope out the conditions and accommodate them. I have multiple orgasms. Four is usually the minimum."

Art stared at her. "Just when I felt cocky."

"Are you interested in trying?" she asked.

"Sure! You heard Pitts, we're back in school to learn as well as teach. But I would like to ask about your friend Richard."

"We fought over exclusivity. He wants it one on one. I can't commit to that."

"So, it will be an open relationship?"

"Yes. Is that okay with you?"

"I think so. Let's see how it goes," he answered, attempting to hide his misgivings. Art remembered his jealousy and the rage that accompanied it many years before, the rage that had resulted in battle and expulsion from high school. Yet, he reasoned, if I don't let her get too close, accept the conditions, whatever she does shouldn't bother me.

They spent the next two weeks together each night at her place. His room and shared bathroom were not compatible with their activities. Some evenings they studied or graded papers, others, she read while he worked on his play. Each night they listened to the Beatles and made love, but he always returned to his room.

Their weekends remained the same, full of beer, games, music and sex. A few times, he started to talk about his play, but she quickly changed the subject, promising she'd read it when he finished. She also resisted his inquiries about her past and her plans for the future.

Despite the emotional distance she sometimes imposed, the times with her were important to Art, respites from his memories of burning flesh, the vacant eyes of the dead, the short-sighted thought process that had reasoned him into the war, all of the horrors that would return for no discernible reason, out of nowhere, alive as though they had just occurred.

When she abruptly stopped inviting him over every night, the pain pierced. On those evenings, she coldly explained that she had other plans. Art knew Richard had returned. Art had seen him on campus and guessed they were together the evenings he didn't see her. Art remembered his internal agreement to compromise, steeled himself, and enjoyed what he had.

On their one-month anniversary, Melanie asked him to spend the night. She bought a cake; they had wine, grass, and great sex.

Late that evening, in a deep sleep with Melanie in his arms, Art's Vietnam dream returned. This dream had started five months before he left Nam and had become a weekly occurrence while he was in country, but since returning to the States, he had only experienced it twice, both during his first week in Norman.

Always the same, Art, covered with sweat hid in the lush jungle from a VC patrol. The night's blackness and the thick grass protected him.

His sweat turned to ice, icicles formed on his chin, and water drops formed on the end of the icicles. The sound of one drop hitting the foliage would cause his death. The patrol passed within yards of him; they knew he hid in the darkness.

One VC soldier stopped within a yard of him. Even in the black night, Art could see the man's sandaled feet. With his AK-47, he parted the grass near Art's head and called excitedly in Vietnamese to his comrades! A drop of water started to fall from Art's chin! Horror coursed through him as it fell in slow motion toward the ground; it pounded the earth like a bomb!

He bolted to a sitting position in Melanie's bed, wet from his sweat. He tried to scream, but his fear did not allow the necessary breath! Over and over, he gasped for air as he tried to let the scream loose! Melanie patted his back, assuring him of his safety. "You're here with me. Everything is fine," she whispered.

After a few minutes, breathing normal, he stood and lit one of her cigarettes.

"Can I do anything?"

In the moonlight, he saw tears running down her checks. "Can you talk about it?"

He turned from her and watched the moon retreat behind dark clouds. "As a kid," he began, "I fought the bullies. Whether they picked on me, my brother or other kids, I fought the bastards. When I went over there, that's how I viewed the war, another fight with the assholes. I don't care how stupid it sounds. That's the way I saw it. After I got there, I learned everything had turned upside down. I'd become the bully, the guy I used to fight, the guy I couldn't stand. Killing another human being is terrible, even if it's for the right reasons. If it's for something else… Jesus!"

He put out the cigarette, dressed and left. For the rest of the night, he wandered the streets of Norman.

Through that evening, Art stayed close to the campus and relived much of his Asian venture. When he left the United States for Vietnam, Art sang the "Ballad of the Green Berets"; when he returned, he sang "Where Have All The Flowers Gone." Like countless men his age, he viewed war as a rite of passage he needed to experience, a way to define self and attain inner strength necessary for the essence of manhood. Fighting communism added righteous zeal to his perception of manifest destiny.

Once there, he witnessed the toll in human life and suffering. More damning, he learned the history that had led America into the ill-fated adventure, and he started to understand the presumptuousness of his unspoken premise: that an entire people, an entire part of the world, had been created to fulfill his quest for manhood.

Art faulted himself for not knowing the facts before he jumped in, but he recognized the difficulty of sorting through the conflicting statements, testimony and theories surrounding the conflict. He also required the shock of the experience to cut through certain values and perceptions society had presented him, at least those he'd accepted.

Early in his tour, Art's view of the history and situation changed through his reading and conversations with Foreign Service Officers who drank and gambled at the International Club in Saigon. CIA spooks who used the Rex Officers Club as their watering hole told him much about the reasons for America's presence. What he learned was neither the versions printed or stated in the American media nor the conventional wisdom offered by the fools on Capitol Hill, at least not by many in the 1960's.

Art's observations and new-found knowledge forged tough questions within him. He knew that paths of glory tied to abstract concepts have been catalysts for young men through the bloody recorded history of human existence to do unnatural things: risk the only lives they possessed and take the lives of others. In Vietnam, he learned that if the abstract concepts are unrelated to the situations on which they are imposed and the fallacy is discovered, the men killing and dying will see themselves as butchers, idiots, or some combination thereof. They will also feel used and betrayed.

As criticism of the war mounted in the States, many Americans who condemned the war labeled the fighting men with various titles, neither acknowledging nor understanding how these men had been duped, forgetting that the act of fighting for one's country had been traditionally considered honorable.

For Art, the demonstrations he witnessed on the Armed Services television in Saigon and read about in papers and magazines increased his ambivalence and isolation. Trapped, he could not condone the war, but neither could he desert his responsibilities or the commitments he had made to the men in his charge.

His disenchantment grew as his relationship with the U.S. Army deteriorated. Its stupidity and total disregard for anything but its own perpetuation amazed him and added to his frustration. Eventually, and ironically, the Army's desire to survive at all costs would lead to the defeat Art concluded must occur.

He'd been in Saigon less than two weeks when he attended a Sunday party hosted by some of the enlisted men who worked for him. They lived downtown at the Duc Hotel, a civilian facility that was rented to the military for enlisted men because of a billet shortage at the MACV compound.

The hotel, six stories high, lodged three men to a room. Art's troops had four rooms on the fifth floor and had invited the rest of the troops to join them in music, American beer, pizza, and what they described as general R&R.

The Duc had the usual fortifications, barbed wire, cement posts in the street and cement guard stands on either side of the main entrance. The wire and cement posts were designed to keep vehicles loaded with explosives from getting too close to the building. The one man on guard duty saluted Art as he entered the hotel lobby.

Inside, Art noted that a disinterested Vietnamese gentleman manned the registration desk. Straight back from the entrance, music blared from the bar and restaurant. One of the working girls spotted Art and walked to the bar's swinging doors. She gave him her most seductive look. "Hey Joe, you buy me Saigon tea?"

He shook his head no.

"C'mon Joe," she pleaded, "I show you good time."

He ignored the second request and headed to the elevator.

"You cheap Charley," she yelled after him. "You number 10."

A huge black Private manned the elevator. "Sir, what floor can I get for you?"

"Fifth, please."

The Private looked concerned. "Sir, are you sure you want the fifth? There's a party up there."

"I know. My name's Patowski. I'm invited."

The Private looked relieved.

Art found his name, and the Private checked it off. "We don't want anyone to wander in who hasn't been invited."

The elevator made it without any trouble. In Vietnam, this meant something. Elevators were not maintained like they are in the U.S. and it wasn't unusual to have one drop a few floors before the safety mechanism kicked in, if it did. Art always considered it an adventure.

On the fifth floor, men stood in the hallway drinking and eating. Some were already passed out on the floor. Groups of men were backed into the hallway out of three rooms, which housed the main attractions. Music and shouting blasted from these rooms. Through the crowd, Art could see beds and parts of naked bodies. He needed to see no more to figure out the entertainment.

Leaving one of these rooms, he ran into Spec 4 Tyronne Morrow, one of his men. "Glad you could make it Lieutenant," Tyronne greeted him. "The place she is a rockin'! See anything in there you like? We have three ladies here to meet your needs, one for each of the major orifices."

Art tried not to look shocked. "Think I'll pass. Looks like some guys had a good time early," he said as they shook hands and surveyed the passed-out troops.

"Don't worry 'bout them. Those Southern boys can't hold their booze or their broads." Tyronne, a tall, lanky black from Detroit, had accepted Art, in part, because of his Chicago background.

"Let me get you a beer," Tyronne offered and led him into a room that looked like a brewery. Large buckets of ice and beer covered most of the floor space, with cases of beer lining the walls from floor to ceiling.

"You guys think you have enough brew?" Art asked laughing.

"Lieutenant, we heard Ho Chi Minh might drop in, and we didn't wanna be caught short." Tyronne cracked a beer and handed it to him. "Now follow me for something you haven't had since you left the land of the big PX."

In an adjoining room, tables lined the three main walls. One contained the remains of standard snack and junk food. The others contained pans of assorted types of pizza. More beer cases were scattered about.

"One of the cooks from the 308th is a buddy of mine. He's from Chi Town and has made the real shit. Chicago pizza, man. Dig in!"

Art grabbed a slice of thin crust pepperoni and nodded his approval to Tyronne. "Great!"

Automatic weapons' fire outside the hotel abruptly interrupted his second bite. He and Tyronne ran out onto the balcony. On the street, an old black Citron had stopped directly in front of the hotel. Blazing automatic weapons extended from the windows and ripped bullets into the front of the building.

The American guard was on the pavement behind the guard stand. Art couldn't tell if he'd been hit.

"Where are your weapons?"

"What weapons?" Tyronne shouted.

"Your rifles, God damn it!"

"Sir, we don't have any fucking rifles! They don't let us keep weapons in the billets."

A number of GIs had run onto the balcony with them.

"Shit!" Art shouted in exasperation. He pushed through the men and into the room, emerging in an instant with two cases of beer. He tore one open and began hurling beer cans at the car. The GIs ran back into the room. Each came back with a case and started throwing beer cans at the car.

Some of the cans grazed the car, which continued to spurt automatic fire into the hotel, stopping only to insert new clips. A couple of cans hit the weapons, which momentarily directed their fire at Art and his beer-toting gang. The instant he saw the barrels of the weapons angle up, Art shouted and grabbed as many of them as he could, pushing them back towards the room.

The bullets hit above and below them, injuring no one. When the weapons retrained on the hotel lobby, Art and the men ventured forward and resumed their beer can attack. They cheered when one of the cans shattered the car's rear window.

The VC retrained their weapons on the beer can throwers. Art and his men retreated, but received no in-coming rounds. Out of ammunition, the VC sped away, screeching around the nearest corner, only fifty feet from the spot where they'd been firing. The men continued throwing beer cans at the car as it rounded the corner on two wheels, almost running head on into an Army jeep with two MPs. Three or four of the beer cans hit the front of the jeep. Those GIs not throwing cans shouted at the MPs and pointed at the escaping Citron.

The MPs, oblivious to everything but the beer cans, sped to the front of the hotel, leaped from their vehicle and raced into the lobby, noticing neither the guard still hugging the pavement, afraid to look up or raise himself, nor the evidence of the recent raid.

They shunned the elevator and ran up the staircase to the fifth floor. When they arrived, red-faced, out of breath, nightsticks drawn, Art greeted them. "Anyone hurt downstairs?" he asked.

"No thanks to you dick heads, throwing fucking beer cans at civilian vehicles!" a huffing Corporal exclaimed. "I'm surprised as hell to find a Lieutenant in the middle of this! How much beer did you guys drink?"

"Corporal, those gooks in the Citron you almost hit must have emptied five hundred rounds into the hotel. Didn't you see the damage downstairs?"

"What're you talking 'bout?" the other MP asked.

He took them outside and showed them the bullet holes.

"Hell, they could've been here for years," one genius replied.

"Look at the plaster and cement on the balcony. For Chris' sake, look at the guard!" Art shouted.

Both MPs saw the guard, just beginning to get up. He looked uninjured.

They were puzzled. "I wondered where he was when we came in," one said to the other.

"Yeah, I didn't even think about it. I was so pissed off 'bout my jeep." He addressed Art. "I just had that fucking jeep painted."

"Let's go down and take a look," Art suggested.

He tried to get them into the elevator, but they insisted it was too dangerous.

In the lobby, the formerly disinterested Vietnamese man, unhurt but badly shaken, jabbered excitedly to an older Vietnamese woman.

The walls and the lobby furniture were riddled with bullet holes. One of the MPs whistled in disbelief. Art, the MPs and Tyronne went into the bar. The girls cried softly, holding one another, occasionally talking through their sobs. A few had minor cuts from shattered glass, but, miraculously, no serious injuries.

The guard, uninjured, explained to Art he wasn't issued live ammunition for his weapon.

After the MPs assessed the damage and took some notes, they all went back upstairs, Art and Tyronne via the elevator, the MPs via the staircase.

They talked to some of the men and inspected the premises. One MP addressed Art. "Lieutenant, considering the circumstances, we'll let the beer throwing go this time, but don't do it again. Make sure the three Vietnamese ladies are out of here too."

"Corporal, why don't these men have weapons?"

Dumbfounded by Art's question, the MP's mouth dropped open, his head slanted to one side. After a moment, realizing Art waited for an answer, he responded. "Sir, this is a war zone. You want someone to get hurt?"

Art served most of his tour in Saigon and might have returned to the U.S. with a few adventures tightly tucked into his head, gotten discharged and continued his life along the linear path he'd started, wrestling with doubts but not faced with major reconstruction of his value system. But in January 1968, the Tet Offensive changed Art's life forever.

Full-fledged battles took place at the MACV compound and in various parts of Saigon. When time and safety permitted, mass graves were dug for the VC dead. The choice was direct: fight or die. The first morning of the offensive, General Westmoreland, on the Armed Forces TV network, declared victory. Unfortunately, the VC weren't watching.

On the seventh day of the offensive, Art tried to make his way to a dispensary in his charge. A block from his destination, he turned a corner and ran directly into a young Viet Cong soldier, trying to escape the fighting.

Less than five feet apart, both froze and looked directly into the other's eyes. Neither saw hatred or anger, only fear.

For a week, both had fired at positions, frontal assaults, vague or blurred targets. Neither had seen the face of any man he'd killed.

Art reacted first, raised his weapon and put five rounds into the young man's chest.

Art stood over the fallen warrior, weapon ready, watching for movement. There was none. Cautiously, he kicked away the dead man's AK 47, bent down and closed his blank, open eyes.

CHAPTER FOUR

ON CAMPUS, Art did not like the daily reminders of the war but watched with interest as protests and anti-war graffiti became commonplace, especially around the ROTC Armory. At a growing rate, groups of students marched around chanting various anti-war slogans. "One, two, three, four, we don't want your fucking war," and "Hey, hey USA, how many kids did you kill today," were favorites.

Despite his attraction to the rebels' idealism, Art suspected many were motivated because they did not want to die or leave the comfort of the familiar. He agreed with the choice of life over death. He simply wished they'd have the balls to say it and not denigrate the choices made by the men and women in Southeast Asia. He also objected to the protesters' distortion of facts and ignorance of history.

He knew their chanting "Ho, Ho, Ho Chi Minh," in support of the dictator was intended to anger the establishment, but it showed no understanding of the history of the situation. Ho was the father of his country, but this did not make him George Washington. How the protesters could ignore or not know that Ho had killed thousands of peasants in a Stalinist type of land reform dismayed Art.

He also understood the motivation of the young men in ROTC uniforms who planned to serve their country. Yet, Art privately faulted them, too, for their lack of historical perspective, believing only what they heard in ROTC classes and from their leaders. Always, he sympathized with their patriotism, remembering himself not many years ago.

If asked his opinion on the war, Art responded from the wellspring of his knowledge, pleasing neither side. His perspective contained too much ambiguity and complexity for those looking for easy answers.

For the majority of students he taught, the war didn't seem to exist, though, often, his classes consisted of men dressed in ROTC uniforms and an equal number dressed in the latest Freddie the Freak outfits or the Okie renditions thereof. Both groups ignored each other. They seemed to exist in their own dimensions. No matter how he tried to get a debate started on any relevant issue, the classes remained indifferent.

He concluded that they lived in a vacuum, aware of only the Rolling Stones, the Beatles and their own hormonal uprisings. This perception helped cushion his feelings of failure, but he didn't surrender to their indifference and continued to press for debate.

A breakthrough finally did occur, but the war, civil rights, or dope didn't ignite this small fire of intellectual controversy and exchange of opinions: the University's fraternity and sorority system did.

In search of a theme topic that might interest them, he asked the class if the University's Greek system would be worth writing about. Most students became excited. Some who had not spoken all semester voiced their disapproval or support. A few thought the fraternity and sorority system had no place on campus; others viewed it as the backbone of the educational process.

The anti-frat group consisted primarily of the long hairs and the anti-makeup ladies. Its leader, a kid Art perceived to be a bright under-achiever, started the discussion.

"The Greek System is an antiquated form of discrimination. It has no place in the college environment, where we're supposed to learn about human rights and freedom of thought."

The ROTC members and their supporters openly scoffed.

"That's crap," one uniformed man retorted. "What have the frats and sororities done to stop human rights. Some of America's greatest thinkers belonged to fraternities."

His followers voiced and nodded their agreement. Other class members laughed.

"How many blacks are in your frat?" the freak leader asked accusingly.

"None now, but we've had some."

"Sure you did, to wait tables and shine shoes."

"Bullshit!" the ROTC man started out of his seat.

"Hey, settle down," Art interjected, stepping between the young men. "Let's keep this on an intellectual level. Give me some of the reasons you joined a fraternity?" he asked the young man ready to fight.

"It helps you get adjusted to college, you meet a lot of people who agree with what you think's important, and after school it helps in the job market."

"What's so wrong with that?" Art asked.

One woman with long hair and no make-up responded. "I don't think you can get the experience with different kinds of people that's important to me. Like he said, in frats and sororities they meet people who think like they do. That's not what I want. I want to hear what other people think about things, people I usually don't talk to or meet."

"Okay," Art said, "There's a qualitative difference worth exploring, diversity of experience."

"Who needs it!" one of the frat men voiced.

"That's what I want to find out," Art responded. "Who values and needs diversity of experience, who doesn't?"

"Whether or not a fraternity or sorority is good or bad is Greek to me," Art continued. The class groaned in unison.

"There's some agreement. But seriously, we've found a topic of interest to most of you. For your next assignment, write a 500 to 600 word theme on whether or not you think the Greek system has any place on campus. Present your thoughts using concrete examples, proof of your position. Don't be afraid to say anything, but have evidence for your statements. Turn the themes in a week from today."

After class ended, he went to his office. He'd just sat down at a desk near the door when a student from the class knocked. She appeared tentative and unsure of herself.

"Professor Patowski, I'm Lauren Longley from the class you just dismissed. I know these aren't your usual office hours, but could I take a minute of your time?"

"Sure, come in."

He took her to the back of the room, as far as he could from three other graduate students in the office.

"This isn't very private, but it will have to do," he apologized. "Next semester I get my own office."

"This is fine," she began. I wanted to ask you about the assignment. A few of us in class don't care about fraternities and sororities. If someone wants to join one, fine, if not, fine."

Art smiled. "That's exactly how I feel."

"But your instructions said to take a position one way or another."

"Any position is fine, including not caring. You can probably present pros and cons about going either way, which would be interesting but more difficult."

A moment of silence ensued as they gazed at each other. She lowered her eyes and blushed. "Thank you, that's probably what I'll do. I've taken too much of your time," she said as she rose to leave.

"Not at all. Come by anytime." He stood and opened his grade book. "You've done well so far."

"Not really," she replied. "One C minus and two Cs."

"That C minus matched the highest grade in class. The Cs resulted from technical problems you need to work through. Your ideas are interesting. They show an unusual maturity."

"I'm older than most freshmen, almost twenty. I spent a year in South Africa on an exchange program through my church."

"South Africa?" he commented in sincere surprise, "A troubled land."

"It is, but Americans are getting only part of the story. They need to know the history of the situation and the Afrikaners' point of view before they make up their mind," she stated with conviction.

"Interesting, that's what I preach about Vietnam, when anyone asks. I hope you'll come back and discuss this with me. It's standard to hear people get excited about Vietnam and U.S. civil rights, but not South Africa."

She looked at the floor. "I'll come during your regular office hours."

Lauren awkwardly held out her hand to shake with him. Smiling, but never looking up, she turned and left.

She appeared for his next scheduled office hours and stayed the entire time, discussing South Africa and her experiences there. After that, at any time during his office hours for the next two weeks, if he didn't have students in for consultation, Art could count on her being there.

They didn't have much privacy during the week, but after he told her he often went to the office on weekends when no one else was around, she started to visit him on Saturdays. He enjoyed the attention, but he genuinely liked her too.

Her arrival in his life coincided with Melanie's departure. From the time of his nightmare, their relationship had deteriorated. She felt uncomfortable with what she'd witnessed. He regretted this, but his anger boiled at being made to feel like a freak.

He'd been back from Vietnam for less than five months, back from a hell most Americans could never understand. For fifteen months he'd lived an existence where life and death walked a thin line. To remain alive required a constant state of alert, a vigilance that created an anxiety all its own. Still, no matter how alert, how smart, nothing could guarantee success: survival. In Nam, being in the wrong place at the wrong time meant all due diligence went for naught.

Returning from this organized chaos, he resented not having time to adjust, time to lose the constant edge he'd developed. He also resented the people around him who didn't care or want to know about the situation. Yet, he recognized most had no frame of reference for his experiences, and he had to co-exist with them.

Art struggled to contain the invisible terror he harbored. For the most part, he'd managed. He could only conjecture as to why the nightmare at Melanie's had occurred, the first time in four months. He thought sleeping in a new environment might have caused it, but he wasn't sure.

She confirmed for him that Richard had returned to her life. This made breaking off easier for both of them. She had a playmate; he did not want to share.

Richard had returned from England with a liberated outlook, or at least he didn't manifest any opposition to competition. Art felt vulnerable. He wanted to fight, but only his internal demons offered conflict.

When Art told Melanie his feelings, she became defensive and warned him about making trouble. He did not know if his distant or immediate past caused her fears, but she cut off his every attempt to explain his frustration. Soon he stopped calling. Their relationship didn't warrant a parting statement. Neither had made a commitment; both had served their purposes.

Thus, to a point, Lauren's arrival on the scene proved fortuitous. Young, pretty and intelligent, she afforded him a degree of feminine companionship, though not the totality he desired.

Art tried to think of her as a child, but her physical attributes made that difficult. At 5' 5" tall, her height resulted from long hips and beautifully formed legs. Her raven hair and dark brown eyes created a Rossetti Pre-Raphaelite beauty. Her large, firm breasts offered an inviting change from the women he'd been with over the past two years.

She fed his ego, viewing him as the knowledgeable teacher whose words she clung to as though they were gold. Her native, naive intelligence delighted him, and Art looked forward to their Saturday conversations. He reasoned she had no interest in him other than academic, that he functioned as an intellectual mentor. But with each meeting, his resolve diminished and sexual fantasies starring the two of them became a regular part of his daily routine.

One mid-October Saturday afternoon, with the Sooner football team playing before a packed Owen Stadium, Art read in his office. The time by which Lauren usually arrived had passed. Disappointed, he didn't expect to see her.

When he heard her footsteps, a smile of anticipation crossed his face, and he turned in his chair to greet her. Standing in the office doorway, her eyes flooded with tears, she said nothing. He sprang to his feet and held her. "What's wrong?" he asked, imagining some unnamable horror.

"After classes yesterday," she sobbed, "I went home. Every Friday my family and I get together and eat at a Mexican restaurant my uncle owns. After dinner, my Mother told me my cat, Dirty Harry, had been run over."

He patted her back in a fatherly manner. She put her head on his shoulder, tears streaming. Relieved to learn no harm had come directly to her but moved by her sorrow, he held her close, trying to lend comfort.

She usually dressed casually for their meetings. This day she wore a pink knit dress that clung to her, accentuating her body's curvature. This awareness started the process of changing fantasy to reality. His penis began its ascent. Art focused all his energy on trying to stop the monster's resurrection. No use!

"Here, why don't you sit down," he said as he disengaged their bodies. He handed her a tissue from the box on his desk and went to his chair, stooping to minimize his bulging pants.

She continued to weep. He rolled his chair to her and held her hands. "I'm sorry. I can only imagine how much you loved him and your sense of loss."

"I guess it's foolish to get so upset about an animal," she said unconvincingly.

"No it's not. They become part of your family. You love them like a sister or brother."

He took another tissue and leaned towards her to blot the tears on her cheeks, their faces inches apart. He moved his mouth to hers; their lips met. His hands went to her breasts, her tongue into his mouth as she made soft moan.

In minutes, trembling from excitement, he asked her to stand as he knelt and raised the dress and slip to her waist. He kissed her legs and pubic hair as he removed her panties. In the process, her dress and slip fell, covering his head. Passion blinded him to the possible dangers from a woman who'd eaten Mexican food the preceding night. Under her dress, cut off from the day, he wrapped his arms around her and hugged her firm softness, taking her scent into his being, not wanting to return to the light.

When he showed no signs of emerging, she tapped his covered head. "Are you all right?" she asked, tears stopped.

Smiling, he uncovered himself, sat in his chair and pulled her down on top of him, stretching out his legs so she could straddle him with her knees and legs. Somehow, his trembling hands managed to insert his penis into her ready, lower mouth.

"My God! We need to close the door!" he realized.

She uttered a small gasp and rose from him to shut the door. Upon returning, she lifted her dress and slid her knees and calves around him in the chair, then expertly lowered herself onto him.

They couldn't manage much movement, but by lifting her butt and lowering it with his hands, he got her to begin a similar motion, allowing him to devote his attention to removing the upper part of her dress, slip and bra. He feasted on her large breasts, alternating them in his mouth, sucking the nipples, licking around them and trying to see how much of both he could get into his mouth at one time.

She pounded hard, oblivious to their surroundings.

As a muted cheer thundered from the stadium for another Sooner touchdown, in the midst of their sexual frenzy, Art's chair splattered into wooden fragments. Both of them landed hard on the floor. The metal part of the swivel base crashed into one wall; a resting arm hit him hard on the side of his head, raising a welt. She received a nasty splinter in her right buttock. Through all of this, Art's penis, ever steadfast, never left her.

Yet, in the tumble, they exchanged positions. On top, ready to continue, chivalry momentarily broke through his lust. "Are you all right?" he asked.

"I'm bleeding."

"Damn!" Art exclaimed, disengaging and helping her stand. He found a bottle of rubbing alcohol in one of the file cabinets and soaked a tissue. She bent over his desk, holding her dress high. He poured alcohol on the wound, and with the tissue extracted the splinter.

He continued to rub her buttock long after he finished his first aid. With his other hand he massaged the other side of her bottom and, ultimately, the furry part between her legs.

She started moving her luscious backside in a circular motion, occasionally thrusting back towards him. He spread her legs slightly and slipped into her from behind.

Though Lauren never fully regained her early passion, Art appreciated that she didn't mind him finishing. While he humped away, she looked at the items on his desk. He'd been reading *Travels with Charley* when she arrived.

Art took her back to his room at Newman Hall where they talked and made love throughout the night. She told him about her home town, Purcell, fifteen miles south of Norman, about her church, mother, and two sisters. Three years before, in her sophomore year in high school, her father had died unexpectedly. He sensed the void this loss had created and her reluctance to discuss it.

Art was thankful that she didn't mind his shabby abode, nor the squeaking bed they exercised. He rented the room for $120 a month and had to share a bathroom. Each time Lauren used it, he ran interference to assure her privacy. He determined that night to find a better, or at least a more private, place to live.

The next morning after breakfast, they returned to his room for more sex. Later, he drove her to her dorm.

Back in his room, sated by the night's activities, he refused to think about the ethics of his situation, unable to rise beyond the pleasure he'd experienced.

CHAPTER FIVE

ART AND MATT WERE INVITED to attend a Monday night football bash, a weekly fall get together that had become legendary.

Carl Pollard, Major, USMC, and commander of the Tulsa Marine Reserve Unit, hosted the event in his apartment.

Carl had returned from Vietnam almost a year before Art and had planned his future with a dedicated focus. Upon completing his Ph.D. in English, he would secure a teaching job near his home in New Mexico, and live a life of tranquillity, contemplating the natural wisdom of Native Americans and leaving the White Man's convoluted conflicts behind.

Although not a Native American, Carl grew up with many of them and shared much of their sensibilities. He had created some controversy in Vietnam by encouraging his platoon to scalp dead VC, a practice that proved effective.

Large and muscular with a thick mustache and a full head of unruly, curly brown hair, Carl appeared mean and rugged. His hair created the impression of an enormous cranial area, leading friends to call him Bullwinkle. They unanimously voiced their expectation that upon graduating, Carl would teach at WossaMatta U.

He greeted Art and Matt at the door. "Welcome, looks like you two came prepared."

"I have two six packs, but dork here thinks he'll get by with one," Matt answered, gesturing toward Art.

"I'm Art Patowski." He extended his hand. "Just trying to impress people with my sobriety."

Carl laughed. "That won't impress any of the wretches here."

He introduced Art to the rest of the Monday night crew. "Here is Brad Cunning, a misnomer if there ever was one."

Art prepared to shake hands with the first of three men seated on Carl's sofa. Brad wore thick glasses, which helped disguise his beady, blue eyes. He wore his blond hair short, a quizzical smile occupying his face.

"Nice to meet you," Art said.

"Don't be kind to him," Carl interjected, stepping between him and Brad. "Note he drinks Falstaff beer. Only 99 cents a six-pack. The cheapest beer on the market. He'll tell you it's out of economic concern for his poor, saintly wife and their children. The truth is he's a cheap prick!"

Brad tried to defend himself but the group's noise silenced him.

A hairy man with a black mustache leaped from a lounge chair and began pounding Cunning with a throw pillow.

The man seated to Cunning's right grabbed another pillow and joined in the bash. Art, laughing, backed away, thinking a riot squad might be needed.

Carl grabbed the men hammering Cunning and pulled them back.

Brad, who had covered his head with both arms during the attack, lowered them. His glasses were knocked side-ways across his face. A large drop of sweat hung from his thick lower lip. The drop of sweat, his trademark, had earned him the moniker *sweat king*, a title he cherished. His goofy smile remained intact.

He straightened his glasses and yelled good naturedly, "Fuck heads!"

The hairy man, Rob DeClines, knew Carl from the Marines. He attended the university to finish his Ph.D. in psychology.

"Rob," Carl explained, "is a sloth in human disguise. He won't move unless it satisfies or fulfills some base self-interest."

"That's nice," Rob replied.

"I met Rob in Officer's Training. Our unit was scaling a cliff by rope. Half way up the mountain the guy in front of me ripped a fart that made my eyes water. The stupid bastard turned around and said 'Excuse me.' It was yours truly," Carl said pointing to Rob, now back in the lounge chair.

"I really was sorry," Rob retorted.

Carl grabbed him by his shirt collar, put a knee into his chest, and leaned on top of him. "These brown eyes were blue till that day!" Carl shouted, punching Rob's right arm with his free fist.

Laughing, Rob tried to grab Carl's fist to stop the plummeting. "You look better with brown eyes," he managed.

They wrestled until Carl released him with a grunt of disgust.

Rick Rouge, or Red Dick, the other crew member who had attacked Cunning, was from New England, married and an enlisted man in Pollard's Reserve unit.

It remained unclear why Red Dick, with a BA from Yale, would attend OU for a masters. Cunning argued that Red Dick had fled the draft and in his haste, had mistaken Oklahoma for Canada.

Rouge offered no explanation and whenever asked about it or anything else, launched into tedious, excruciatingly boring stories in a monotone designed to induce instant sleep. After hearing him drone on for ten minutes, Art decided Rick's mother had mated with a tsetse fly.

The other places in the group were floating memberships occupied by different men. This variance in attendance resulted from difficulty some invitees had with the mayhem that occurred throughout the evening, especially in the fourth quarter after much liquor had been consumed.

Each attendee put five dollars into a pool, took the team of his choice and the points by which he thought the team would win. Because no one had any money, winning the pool meant more than bragging rights, but bragging rights were the main incentive.

This night the first half stayed relatively tame, ending with the Packers ten points ahead of the Redskins.

At the break, all the men journeyed to the nearest liquor store. Rob bought a bottle of Uzo, a potent licorice-flavored Greek liquor. The others replenished their beer supply. By the fourth quarter, Rob had everyone who'd bet on the Redskins drinking a shot of Uzo each time they gained a first down.

Matt had finished his two six-packs before the end of the first half and had picked up two more, one of which he finished by the end of the third quarter. He'd bet on the Redskins and enjoyed the Uzo washed down by his dwindling supply of beer.

With less than thirty seconds left to play, the Redskins took the lead.

Cunning leaped into the air. "I've got the Skins by two. Give me that money!"

He raced to the kitchen bar and gathered the pool money into his pocket.

"You're losers! All losers!" he shouted, taking another shot of Uzo.

McGaw had the Skins by one. When they made the extra point for the two point lead, he downed a double shot of Uzo and shouted blurred obscenities at Cunning. Then he lay in the middle of the room, stared at the ceiling and mumbled, rapidly leaving the realm of the intelligible.

The rest of the group, disheartened, told Cunning what they thought about him, his ancestry and his relationship with his mother.

He sat back down on the sofa laughing, slapping the pocket where he'd put the money. "Losers! Who'd you think you're messing with? Losers!"

The Redskins tried to put the ensuing kickoff through the end zone for a touchback, but the ball fell short and into the arms of a Packer.

He started straight up the field. At the fifteen yard line, he broke to his left, avoiding a would-be tackler. At the thirty, two Redskins converged on him, but a blocker appeared from nowhere, cutting the nearest Redskin down, allowing the runner to cutback right; the other Redskin dove at him but tackled only air.

The second cutback enabled the Packer blockers to take care of the remaining Redskins. The runner saw a seam and took it. At the Packer forty-yard line, only the Washington kicker stood between him and the goal line.

Cunning leaped to his feet along with everyone but McGaw. "Cut that fucker down!" Cunning screamed.

"Go, go, go!" the others yelled.

The runner gave the kicker his right leg, then did a pirouette worthy of Baryshnokov, freezing the kicker, who could only turn and futilely chase him.

He raced into the end zone as the final gun sounded.

The group in Pollard's living room ignited! Rob raised the ottoman over his head and hurled it full force at Cunning. The two pillows used earlier to pound him were enlisted for the same purpose.

Cunning curled into the sofa and covered up. Art, who had won the pool, threw magazines at him.

"Who's the Loser? Loser! Loser!" the group shouted, beating him with the ottoman, pillows and magazines.

"Give me my money you asshole!" Art yelled, on his feet, pounding Cunning with Pollard's latest issue of *Playboy*.

Cunning faced the back of the sofa, both hands and arms protecting his head, with his knees curled up to his chest. He managed to loosen one hand and dig into the pocket where he'd put the money. He then hurled it behind him towards the group.

"Yeah! Yeah!" Pollard, Rob, and Red Dick shouted, holding their weapons above their heads.

The two men not participating in the riot had made their way to the door, laughing uneasily, but trying to look as though they were in the spirit of the donnybrook.

Cunning's release of the money froze the frenzy. The crew watched Art pick the dollars off the floor, voicing their approval.

A loud gurgling sound diverted their interest.

Matt, in the midst of the mayhem, had passed out lying on his back. A fountain of barf erupted from his mouth, shot a foot into the air, and descended straight back down onto his face and into his open mouth.

He coughed and choked as another gusher that went higher than the first greeted the returning vomit.

"Jesus!" Cunning yelled, "It's Old Faithful."

All stared in riveted disgust. The second emission went straight back into Matt's mouth, exacerbating his choking.

Pollard looked at the entourage. "Hey guys, he's going to suffocate. Someone should do something."

"It's not my apartment," Red Dick countered.

Matt let go another blast that Saint Helens would have envied. Again, the corruption fell directly back into his face and mouth. Unconscious and too drunk to move, he lay gagging, thrashing his arms and legs around in a puddle of his own regurgitated crud.

Cunning and Art ran to him. Brad pulled Matt to a sitting position and hit his back to knock the vomit from his mouth and throat. Art ran to the bathroom and grabbed some towels to clean Matt's face. His shirt and hair were matted with vomit, but Cunning's actions had stopped the choking.

"See you guys tomorrow," the two silent ones said, leaving without venturing another glance at Matt.

Pollard soaked more towels and tried to clean the mess on his carpet.

With the vomiting subsided, Cunning and Art were able to clean Matt's face and, to some extent, his hair and shirt.

They carried him outside, Art with one of Matt's arms around his neck, Cunning the other. As they prepared to dump him into the front seat of Art's VW, Pollard emerged from his apartment with an open can of beer and his Marine Corp sword. Rob and Red Dick stood behind him.

"Wait!" Pollard exclaimed. Standing in front of the still unconscious Matt, he placed the can above Matt's head and poured beer onto his matted hair. Placing his sword on Matt's right shoulder he proclaimed, "I christen thee Lava King, and from this day forward that is how ye shall be known."

Some of the beer dripping from Matt's head found its way into his mouth. Matt, eyes locked shut, smacked his lips, smiled, then shot out a stream of barf that scored a direct hit on Pollard's chest.

"Shit, get more towels," Art moaned.

Matt's wife, Virginia, met them at the door, unhappy.

"Can you get him into the bedroom?" she asked. "Every time I see the two of you together he's in this condition," she directed at Art.

He remained silent, struggling to get the dead weight into bed, anxious to leave.

"What kind of booze did you feed him tonight?"

"Virginia," Art retorted, "I didn't feed him anything. He drank what he wanted to of his own accord."

"Sure. Tell me he didn't get a lot of encouragement."

Art decided not to argue.

As they deposited Matt on the bed, Virginia's cat, Fred, leaped onto his chest, claws out.

"Yeow!" Matt yelled half-raising himself in his stupor and grabbing for the cat, long gone.

"You miserable fucker! I'll kill ya!" he screamed, trying to raise himself, but falling back onto the bed. "Damn bitch and her fucking cat! I hate both you miserable pussies!" From his prone position, Matt swung his fists as though he were fighting.

"Are you all right?" Art asked Virginia.

"I'll be fine," she responded. Her eyes gave a different answer.

Art and Brad waited in the hallway for a few minutes. When Matt's motions and mumbling stopped, they left.

"That looks like a bad scene," Art offered in the car.

"Yeah," Brad responded. "I hope it's just the booze."

CHAPTER SIX

POLLARD'S DUPLEX APARTMENT had two bedrooms, and for economic reasons he needed someone to share the bills.

The rent, more than double what Art paid at Newman Hall, hurt financially, but with the apartment he'd have reasonable privacy when Lauren visited and a bathroom he shared with one person, not one floor. Thus, with no hesitation, Art said yes when Carl asked if he were interested.

Pollard's schedule added to the attractiveness of the move. As Commander of the Tulsa Marine Reserve unit, he left Norman Friday afternoon to be in the Tulsa office Saturday and Sunday. He spent Friday, Saturday and Sunday nights with a transplanted Texan, Clare Swift, returning to Norman Monday morning in time to teach his 9:00 class.

Art's first Friday night in the apartment, he drove to Purcell and waited for Lauren outside the Baptist Youth Center on Main Street.

She emerged alone. Spying him, she raced to the car.

"Let's get out of here," she said, quickly closing the door behind her.

"Any trouble getting away?"

"No one saw me leave the Center, and Mom thinks I'm spending the weekend in the dorm. I should be okay."

"Good," he responded. "You look terrific."

She wore white shorts and an OU sweat shirt. With the car safely in gear, he reached over with his right hand and rubbed the inside of her nearest leg, massaging it just up to the hem of her shorts. She didn't object.

In less than five minutes, he turned the car onto the interstate. She placed his free hand on her crotch.

"I don't know if I can make it to Norman," he said in anguish, his pants bulging.

"You know this place. Isn't there anywhere we can stop?" he pleaded.

Lauren looked in front and behind them. The highway appeared almost deserted. "We can make do."

Placing his hand on the steering wheel, she put her left arm behind his seat and massaged his penis with her right hand.

After a second, he placed her right hand on the steering wheel to guide the car and unzipped his pants, freeing his straining member. He then released her hand from the steering wheel, placed it on his exposed penis, and continued driving. She accommodated with a gentle up and down stroke. "Couldn't do it better myself," he thought.

After a minute, he looked in the rear view mirror. One truck remained some distance behind them, but no vehicles were in front of them.

"Baby, this is nice, but I know something even better," he recommended. Without taking his eyes off the road, Art put his right hand behind the nape of her neck and lowered her mouth to his waiting member.

In order for her to take his full measure and to refrain from hitting her head on the steering wheel, Art moved his seat back. Between this effort, which made him stretch his leg to reach the accelerator, and entering the pangs of ecstasy, which made him forget on what planet he lived, their speed decreased to forty miles an hour.

The truck he'd seen in the rear view mirror soon passed them.

As it went by, Art's eyes met those of a man seated in the cab on the passenger side. His vague disinterest changed to excited agitation when he saw Lauren swallowing Art's cock.

The man whirled to tell the driver his discovery just as the truck left the passing lane to pull in front of them. The driver, his hands still on the wheel, turned 180 degrees to get a peek at the festivities, causing the truck to swerve violently to the right. The driver's actions created a violent rocking motion. Before he made another adjustment, the truck's right front wheels hit the shoulder gravel and skidded into the softly-sloped ditch next to the shoulder, crashing onto its side.

Art, reluctantly, disengaged Lauren from his prized part while he maneuvered his car into the far lane to safely pass the wrecked truck.

"Oh, Oh my goodness! What happened!" she exclaimed, seeing the truck lying on its side, wheels still spinning.

"I think a drunk truck driver lost control," Art said getting past the scene as quickly as possible.

"Shouldn't we stop?"

"No, I'm sure they're all right. They didn't hit that hard, and there's no fire. Don't worry about it," he said, patting her leg.

She turned back, anxiously looking at the wreck.

"Relax, just keep this going and everything will be fine," he said taking her hand and placing it on his unrepentant, still upright penis.

When they got to Norman, he took her to a small, deserted park and stopped in a secluded area.

"How do you know this place, Arthur?"

He hated to be called Arthur. "I coached little league here."

"You are wonderful."

He felt stupid, sitting exposed, trying to find a way to ask her to finish what they'd started on the highway. "Would you mind terribly?" he implored, glancing at his groin. "Then maybe we can get a pizza."

"Oh, sure, hors d'oeuvres," she responded, taking her long dark hair in her left hand and bending over. Minutes later they were on their way to Orin's.

Campus corner glowed with neon and the vibrancy of young souls pursuing their bliss. Jim, the acid freak, a fixture on the corner, wearing only cutoffs, radio blaring, sat crossed-legged on the sidewalk outside the Town Tavern, stoned on something, his German Shepherd at his side.

The English Department's janitor strolled among the masses shouting, "Repent, repent ye sinners and be saved!" as he handed pamphlets to anyone who'd take them. Young couples waited outside the Boomer Theater for the next showing of *Easy Rider*. Students walked leisurely, window shopping and people watching.

Inside Orin's, Lauren excused herself while he ordered. He didn't see Melanie until she stood a few feet from the table.

"Hello," she said, Richard at her side.

"How are you, stranger?" he asked, surprised at seeing her.

"Fine, how about you?"

"Great, have a seat."

She sat across from him, Richard next to her. "Richard, Art, Art, Richard." she nodded toward both men. They mumbled hello, neither excited about meeting the other.

The waitress arrived with a pitcher of beer and two glasses.

"Would you mind getting a couple more glasses?" Art asked.

"We can only stay a minute. We were just leaving," Melanie offered.

"Where have you been?" he asked her.

"Around, we've been hanging out, enjoying the sights and sounds."

"I haven't seen you in the office."

"I've only been making the classes I teach."

The waitress and Lauren arrived at the same time. After introductions, Melanie and Richard quickly drank their beers and left. She glanced back at him once, as Richard held the door open for her.

Nothing had happened, but he felt terrible. Outside of a few glimpses on campus, he hadn't seen her for nearly a month.

"Is something wrong?" Lauren interrupted his reverie.

"No, why do you ask?"

"You seemed sad."

"It's the beer. Weak 3.2 beer always makes me pensive."

"Makes you sad?" she asked, not certain of his intent. Her question broke through his gloom.

Laughing, he took the small candle on their table, held it at eye level, then blew it out. "Out, out brief candle…"

"Arthur," she teased, taking his hand, "your wick is endless. It will never go out."

"Be quiet Lauren," he laughed, "or all these ladies will want to date me."

They arrived at the apartment early. He enjoyed not having to worry about neighbors or bathroom arrangements.

"Who lives next door?" she asked.

"An old guy. He's retired from the military. I haven't met him, but Carl says he's nice. That reminds me, we have to leave the bedroom curtains open an inch or two."

"Why?"

"If Carl or I have overnight lady visitors, we let him watch, provided he doesn't take pictures. At the end of the month he buys us a bottle of scotch. If he's enjoyed the entertainment, we get Chivas, if he hasn't, Cutty Sark."

"Oh Arthur, you're pulling my leg," she responded, turning away.

"No! I think we'd better get started," he took her in his arms. "I'm sure you'll make this a Chivas month." They sat together on the bed and kissed.

"You tease too much," she said. Sometimes I don't know when to believe you."

He pulled her down next to him. The bed felt soft and smelled clean. "I can't believe it. A real bed, mattress, everything. Do you have to do anything, I mean birth control?"

"I went on the pill the month before school started."

"You had plans," he said lightheartedly.

"I thought it the responsible thing to do. In light of what's happened between us, I guess it was. Even though I was a virgin, I thought I'd experiment," she said never making eye contact. She stood and put her overnight case on the dresser.

"Lauren, you are kidding? You're not saying you were a virgin when we made love in my office, right?"

She pulled a nightgown from the case, still not looking at him. "Yes, Arthur, you're my first man."

"Well, there must have been a hell of a lot of boys," he laughed.

She sat on the bed and cried, covering her eyes with the gown. "I don't know how you can say a terrible thing like that."

He sat next to her and put his arm around her.

"Hey, take it easy. It's fine. I didn't mean to sound judgmental. You surprised me when you said I was first."

"Well, you were."

"Okay," he responded, confused, wondering why she would lie. Art felt uneasy, concerned that he was missing something about her expectations.

"You don't believe me," she said, still crying.

"I said not to worry." He held and kissed the nape of her long neck.

She turned to him. "Please kiss me, Arthur."

For the first time, he recognized how much child remained in this woman's body. He kissed her, then turned off the bedroom light. That night, they did not play.

He awakened to the smell of bacon and coffee. In the kitchen, Lauren scurried between the refrigerator, stove and table. For a minute, he silently watched, marveling at her efficiency. She jumped when she saw him.

"I didn't hear you get up. How do you like your eggs?"

"Any way is fine. Where'd you get the food?"

"I ran over to Safeway."

"Jesus! You shouldn't spend any money.

"Nonsense, Arthur. It didn't cost much."

"Really, you shouldn't," he responded, heading for the bathroom. "Give me a minute, and I'll be back."

When he emerged, she had a full breakfast ready.

"I hope you like English muffins?" she asked, watching for his reaction. He felt awkward at the attention.

"Very much, but don't spend your money. In fact, I'll pay you for this."

"Arthur, you will not."

He reached across the table and took her hand. "Please, do not call me Arthur," he said evenly, but firmly.

She bowed her head. "You don't like Arthur? It's such a beautiful name."

"Arthur's fine. I just prefer Art. Arthur reminds me of the Fisher King, the impotent one from Eliot's *The Wasteland*, the one whose problems cause the blight on the land."

"I don't know the poem," she responded. "When I hear the name, I think of King Arthur."

"I can see why I remind you of King Arthur. We have so much in common."

"You do. Warrior, scholar, leader of men. Besides, I don't think you have to worry about impotence," she said, the hint of a smile around the corners of her mouth.

"At least not with you around to inspire me." He kissed her hand and released it.

The remainder of the morning they prepared for a picnic at Lake Thunderbird, about twenty miles east of Norman.

When they arrived at the lake, the chill had kept all but a few hearty souls away. They found a secluded spot and set up camp.

"We almost have the place to ourselves, but it's not that cold," he commented, trying to convince himself more than her.

They unfolded a blanket and placed it on the ground. He opened a bottle of wine and poured for them.

"Here's looking at you kid," he toasted as they huddled together. "When I first came to Norman, this place didn't exist. That was ten years ago. You were nine. Did you ever get out here?"

"No, we'd occasionally go to Norman to shop, but we never got this far east. When did you first see OU?"

"Some buddies at the Air Base suggested going to see Oklahoma play Kansas State. Back then, they called the Big Eight Oklahoma and the seven dwarfs. The guys figured we'd be able to get seats to that game. K State's bad now; in those day they were worse. OU won 61-6."

"Must have been an off day for the Sooners," she joked.

"Very good, and you're right."

"What did a Chicago boy think of Norman in those days?"

"Ten years doesn't seem that long ago," he commented. "I fell in love with the town, or with what I imagined it to be. After the game, we walked around the campus and campus corner. The ivy-covered red brick buildings, the relaxed, friendly atmosphere, the people, the coeds, everything seemed so perfect, the antithesis of Chicago and the Air Force. I knew it couldn't be Utopia, but I enjoyed the mirage, like a pleasant dream I kept alive by not waking. I decided then and there, I'd go to school in Norman. Didn't even have a high school education at the time, but I'd go to OU."

"You had a dream and made it come true. You were right about the people. They are good."

Art looked at her, trying to determine the strength of her conviction. "Oklahomans combine Midwestern virtue and Southwestern self-reliance, but early on, after starting school, when I heard Okies brag about Norman not allowing blacks on city streets after sundown, I knew I hadn't found paradise."

"They had to grow up like a lot of people."

"True, or maybe they were worried about blacks getting run over because they blended into the night so well. These people are pragmatic, just like Chicagoans. If it works, don't fix it, but if change is inevitable, blend it in as painlessly as possible."

"Is that wrong?"

"Not necessarily. But often, there's a hypocrisy in the process that bothers me. They don't do something because it's right, but because it's less trouble than the alternative. I'm not sure the underlying attitudes change."

"But with it comes the chance for people to interact and learn about one another," she insisted.

"And really hate each other," he added.

"You're such a pessimist. Why can't it go the other way?"

"It can," he conceded. "There's at least an I-It relationship created that has a chance to become an I-Thou relationship. The way things have been here, in Chicago, other places, blacks, anyone different, haven't even had a chance to be an It."

"Our first black family moved into Purcell when I was fifteen," Lauren commented.

"How'd it go?"

"Not well. One of the boys in the family was a junior at the high school. He played football, but the boys on the team gave him a terrible time."

"Of course they did," Art interjected: "He had the biggest dick in school. That pissed those good ol' boys off."

"Arthur, you shouldn't make jokes like that," she scolded.

"Who's joking, and you called me Arthur again." He put his arms around her. "We're going to have to devise a penalty for each time you call me Arthur. I have something in mind. It's like washing your mouth out for saying a bad word, but you don't use soap."

Lauren didn't smile. "That's fine, just so we have a penalty for you when you say something naughty."

He pulled her down to the blanket. "If what you have in mind is reciprocal, I won't consider that punishment."

"Then we'll have to think of something else," she responded, a smile breaking through. They kissed as he slipped his hand inside her jacket and under her sweater.

"Let's get behind one of the trees," he suggested.

"There are people here," she protested.

"They're too far away to see us, especially if we go behind one of the trees."

"No, it's too public."

"You want to, don't you?" he asked.

"Yes, but..."

"We'll go past the trees into that tall grass. No one can see us there," he interrupted.

They walked to the grass, and he made a small enclave. Seated on the blanket, Lauren took off her jeans. He unzipped his pants, ready to proceed. She took him, shivering but wanting to please. Goose bumps rose on her body. "Art, c... could y... you p... please h... hurry. I'm free... freezing," she pleaded.

"Just a second more," he panted.

Without warning, Art felt a wet, cold sensation on his anus. He pulled out of Lauren, whirled around on his knees and came face-to-face with a basset hound. Before Art could react, the hound looked to the heavens and produced a mournful howl. Art heard the grass on one side parting and the sound of someone walking towards them. Lauren struggled to get into her clothing. He had difficulty fitting his bulging member back into his pants.

"Demetrius, Demetrius, where are..." Before the young woman finished her call, she saw Lauren, Art and her dog. Art held both hands in front of his still excited penis while Lauren wrestled with her jeans. The hound cut loose another pitiful wail.

"Demetrius, come here," she called, turning side ways to avoid the scene, but then looking back at Art. They recognized each other from the English Department.

Fully tucked in, Art grabbed the dog and carried it to the woman. "I didn't do anything. He just started howling."

She cradled the dog, keeping her eyes turned, then walked away. After a few steps, she called back: "See ya around campus." Her laughter echoed off the lake water.

He helped Lauren to her feet. "Let's eat lunch at home."

CHAPTER SEVEN

All English Graduate Assistants were asked to attend an Emergency Meeting in Kaufmann Hall, home to the English Department.
Art rode to the meeting with Pollard, who'd finessed a faculty parking sticker.

"What do you suppose this is about?" Art asked.

"I understand they're expecting trouble, some kind of anti-war activity," Carl answered.

"What the hell do they expect us to do about it? My students are only interested in things that directly affect them, like staying in school to stay out of the war."

"That's been my experience too," Carl concurred. "I think we'll be told to be careful and not fuel any controversy. They've received threats."

"How do you know all this? Nora's telling you, isn't she? When you're around she makes cow eyes, and now that we're roomies, I'm one of her best friends. Are you getting any of that?" he asked laughing.

"Not funny, dip-shit," Carl responded as they pulled into the parking lot.

Art had learned that Nora, one of the Department secretaries, was unhappily wed to an Iranian and mad about Carl. Art thought her unhappy marriage proved the truth of Kipling's warning about east and west never meeting. He often saw bruises on her arms and neck. Twice, her make-up could not disguise black eyes.

Art noted that while Carl was always friendly and considerate when talking to Nora, he had managed the relationship carefully to assure it stayed platonic. Nora interpreted Carl's refusal to get physical with her as another sign of his integrity.

"Hey," Art continued, "The only thing keeping her and her three kids from eternal bliss with the man she worships is her corn-holing, swarthy rag-head husband. She bumps him off, and the coast is clear."

Carl glared at Art as they got out of the car. "As I said, not funny. Be careful what you say to her. She's desperate enough to do something really stupid."

They arrived at the meeting room five minutes early. Cunning, seated with Red Dick and Matt, had saved seats for them.

Art, to no avail, scanned the room for Melanie.

At 7, Pitts appeared with Dr. Eldka, head of the English Department. Pitts appeared to be in better shape than at any time Art had seen him. He stood behind the lectern for a full minute, but the noise from the crowd didn't subside. Recognizing courtesy would not prevail, he started.

"Please, please, Ladies and Gentlemen, let's have some quiet so we can begin. I appreciate each of you taking your own time to come this evening. A few unusual matters have arisen which require communication with all of you. Dr. Eldka will spend a few minutes addressing these matters. Then we'll try to answer any questions you might have."

Dr. Eldka, a tall thin man with gray hair, stood to address them.

"Hello. I haven't met each of you, but I'm certain in the near future I will. Usually, I don't formally address the Graduate Assistants. Dr. Pitts has been doing this job for five years; he calls it his term in purgatory, and is totally capable of handling any items that arise. However, because of the unusual circumstances we're facing and about to discuss, I asked him if he'd mind my saying a few words.

"As we all read and hear daily in the media, there's a growing protest movement concerning America's involvement in Southeast Asia. Much of the protest movement, for good or ill, has been centered in various universities around the country. Here, we've not had too much activity, some picketing around the ROTC Armory, letter-writing to the school newspaper, but nothing as dramatic as the activities at Berkeley or Columbia. We hope events here do not get to that point, and in saying that I'm not being political. I'm simply alluding to the shut down of what most of us think the university's main purpose is: the open discussion of ideas, whether those ideas concern the theory of fiction or the politics of Southeast Asia.

"Unfortunately, some people are not interested in discussion. During the last week, there have been a number of letters and a few telephone calls that suggest our campus is a target for some type of action. Specifically named are the ROTC facilities, the newspaper and the English Department. How and why we managed to make this list puzzles me, although I am happy to report that both sides think we're on the other side. In some of the communication we've been called commies, pinkos, fascists or Nazis.

"While I'm pleased with the balance these allegations suggest, my limited math skills inform me our chances for having an incident are increased."

He smiled at this humor and the audience returned some uneasy laughter.

"Therefore, we're asking you to be sensitive to the situation and conduct your classes in a manner that will not fuel emotions in this delicate area."

Before he said another word, Rod Show, a fourth-year graduate student, leaped to his feet. "Dr. Eldka, are you asking us to discontinue any discussions we're having in our classes regarding the war?" His tone suggested more of an accusation than a question. Rod remained standing.

"Not at all," Eldka responded. "I'm simply recommending that each of you be sensitive to the volatility of this issue, and when any such discussions occur in your classrooms, assure that you give all sides equal opportunity and not fuel the debate. We have to take the threats seriously."

"What about expressing our opinions?" Rod countered.

"Again, I'm asking you to be sensitive to the highly emotional attitudes surrounding the war. Whether or not you want to use the classroom as a forum for your individual political views is an issue that each of you must determine for yourself. I, personally, am skeptical about the value of pursuing these issues in Freshman English. However, academic freedom is a valued quality that can take many forms. Again, each of you must decide certain questions for yourself. Just remember, many people, including your students, see you as representatives of the university. Each of you should be certain the students understand you speak for yourself, not the university."

"Perhaps we should read a disclaimer before every discussion," Rod continued.

"Give it a rest!" Matt called out. Others, including Art and Brad voiced their impatience. Rod finally sat down.

Eldka raised his hands for quiet. "This is a perfect example of the emotion this issue engenders. No one in this department is telling or asking you to refrain from anything. I'm informing you of the sensitivity surrounding our situation and asking you to use common sense in your handling of any and all matters, which is what we've always asked. Are there any questions on this?"

"Does anyone know how serious the threats are?" one student asked.

"The FBI is investigating them. As of this morning, they do not think we have too much to worry about. They are, however, increasing security where necessary," Eldka answered. "None of these activities should be apparent to you. No one will be in your classes who shouldn't be there. But they'll have plainclothes agents walking around, and I think they'll be more uniformed officers too."

"Will they be taking names?" Rod called, not standing this time.

"No. They're not here to monitor activity. They're here to prevent a bomb from exploding. That was promised to the faculty senate and is a matter of public record. They will be here to avoid trouble, not cause it."

There were no more questions.

"Thank you all. In parting, let me add that we're not asking anyone to do anything out of the ordinary. Just use discretion. If you notice anything unusual, report it to the department office. I'll turn the rest of the meeting over to Dr. Pitts." He sat and Pitts addressed them.

"Since we're all here, there's one item I want to mention. Next Tuesday, the Oklahoma Coalition for the Arts will have its annual Norman meeting. It will be held at 6:00 PM in room 204 in the student union. As some of you know, they solicit work in any genre and medium. They'll provide money in the form of grants to aspiring artists. One of our students, Mr. Show, received such a grant, which led to his winning an O'Henry short fiction prize."

After a few general questions about the Council, the meeting adjourned. Art, Carl, Brad, Matt and Rick headed for the pub at the student union. As they left the room, Art encountered the woman whose dog had happened upon him and Lauren at the lake.

"Hello," she greeted Art, laughing.

"Oh boy," he responded. "I'd seen you around the Department, but I didn't know you were a teaching assistant.

"Hi Carl," she greeted Pollard.

"Hello Judith. I see you know my new roomie."

"We haven't been formally introduced, but he and my dog Demetrius are intimate friends."

"I'm Art Patowski," he extended his hand. "Tell Demetrius he should do something about that cold nose."

Her laughter reminded him of the lake.

"What's this all about?" Carl asked, puzzled.

She regained her composure and took Art's hand. "I'm Judith Hunter." She looked at Carl, "He can explain all of this, but," she continued, addressing Art, "if you don't tell on Demetrius, I won't tell on you."

"I'll think about it."

She waved and walked away, still laughing.

At the student union, the men found a vacant booth and ordered beers.

"Okay, what gives with you and Judith?" Carl asked Art.

"To make a long story short, last Saturday a young lady and I were getting to know each other pretty well out at Lake Thunderbird when Judith's dog stuck his nose up my ass."

"You're kidding! She caught you in the act?"

"Actually, her dog did, but I don't want to talk about it. Both of them probably love me."

"You were hosing this chick in broad daylight?" Matt asked.

"We were in tall grass," Art explained. "Guys, you have to go for the gusto when the spirit moves you."

"Which for you is most of the time," Brad commented.

After the laughing quieted, Brad asked them what they thought of the meeting.

"I don't think there's much to worry about," Art responded. "I can't see this campus joining the twentieth century for at least another hundred years."

"My wife, Virginia, for those unfortunates who haven't met her, works in the Bursar's office," Matt started. "The scuttlebutt there is that the SDS is working the campus trying to gain some enthusiasm for their point of view. Their reputation isn't good."

"What's the SDS?" Rouge asked.

"Red Dick, do you ever read anything that's not literary?" Brad asked. "SDS is the Students for a Democratic Society. They've led demonstrations and have been accused of blowing up a few buildings. They're in the papers a lot."

"Yeah," Matt agreed, "Some heavy duty shit."

"And I thought I was getting away from the war," Art injected.

Carl grunted. "Not that easy, my friend. Crazies are everywhere."

"Speaking of crazies, what'd you guys think of that jerk giving Eldka a bad time?" Matt asked.

The others shrugged their shoulders, noncommittal. "He got a bit boring, but his point's well taken," Art offered.

"Show's not crazy," Carl stated. "I got to know him last year, and he has some original ideas. They're different, but worth listening to. The award he won is no joke. I've read some of his fiction. It's damn good."

"Well guys, speaking of fiction, I've got to hit the books," Matt said, drinking the last of his beer.

"Lava King leaving after one beer! There is going to be a revolution!" Art exclaimed.

"Man, I have the frigging qualifying exam next week. Any of you guys taking it?"

"I am," Rouge answered.

Art, Carl and Brad had already qualified at the Ph.D. level, Rouge at the M.A.

"You guys will do fine. Just memorize the Literary Handbook and read everything ever written in British and American literature, including everything that's ever been written about everything written," Brad offered.

"Thanks much," Matt and Rick groaned.

"I have the Master exams in November. They should be fun," Art offered.

"Are they after Thanksgiving?" Brad asked.

"The week after. Perfect timing to screw up the holiday."

"Not totally, I hope," Brad offered. "I'm inviting all you guys, your wives, special friends, to our house for Thanksgiving. We do the traditional thing every year, and there should be football on the tube. Bring your beer and a good appetite. Can Clare make it in from Tulsa?" he asked Carl.

"If she has Friday off, probably. The Corps won't be meeting that weekend, so I'll definitely be there. In case she asks, will there be any sweat on the turkey?"

"Hey, Marilyn's really looking forward to seeing her. If she shows up without you, fine. I assume you guys will bring your wives," Brad addressed Matt and Rick.

"Unless I get a better offer, which isn't likely," Matt responded. Rick nodded his assent.

"How about you Art, bringing the lady of the lake?"

"She'll probably be with her family, but I'll ask Judith if Demetrius can make it."

CHAPTER EIGHT

PITTS' COMMENTS about possible financial help prompted Art to attend the Oklahoma Council for the Arts meeting. His play nearly completed, he hoped assistance with a stage production might be obtained.

Over two hundred students attended, many older graduate students. From the stains on much of their clothing, Art guessed the majority were painters. He sensed an underlying current of energy he didn't understand.

Skippy Steers, the Council's Director, decked out in his best Okie mod, maroon leisure suit, off blue-colored shirt, four-inch-wide white patent leather belt and white patent leather shoes, started by introducing the six Council members seated behind him on stage and explaining the Council's structure.

"All the major metropolitan areas are represented. A true cross section of the state," he said with pride.

"A real cosmopolitan group!" a voice from the audience yelled.

Skippy's chest puffed out. "Well it ain't no New York City, but we thank the Almighty for that."

Scattered applause brought a smile to Skippy's round face.

"Each council member," he continued, "is college-educated and active in the arts in their community. This is my first full term as Director of the Council, though I've served on it for six years, but we're going to handle things like before. Those of you who want to participate in the visual arts need to send representative work to council members at the time and place indicated in the instructions, which you can pick up as you leave the meeting. Are there any questions?"

One student wearing a headband and paint smudged T-shirt raised his hand. "How do you judge entries?"

"Well, depending on what it is," Skippy started, "we look at it or read it. For written work, we jot down our thoughts and send them to the Council secretary who distributes them to all Board members. We have to have our writing to her at a stated time, and she must distribute the collected writings in a timely manner. At a subsequent meeting, we all vote on whether or not to pursue a submission.

"Painting and handicrafts are handled different. We'll ask artists to display their work at particular times and furnish the letter I mentioned before. We try to make this as inexpensive as possible. After the exhibits, the same process takes place as with written stuff."

"What kind of work are you looking for?" one student asked.

"We're looking for quality," Skippy responded.

"But are there things you'll automatically reject?" another asked.

"We want good taste and judgment. That's the only criteria I can think of," Skippy answered.

"Would a painting of Governor Bartlett in panty hose be acceptable?" someone from the audience asked.

Skippy laughed. "I donno; if you got one, I'd like to see it."

"Hey Skippy, you got a thing about boys in panty hose?" another student yelled.

Skippy's demeanor darkened. Before he could respond, another member of the audience yelled, "No, just boy Republicans in panty hose."

Skippy, frowning, raised his hands for silence. "We're here to encourage and maybe help some of you financially. We don't need this abuse!"

"Yeah, you've abused yourself enough already!" someone yelled.

The noise increased. "Is it true that to be a council member your parents had to be siblings?" another student called. Skippy and the other council members looked uneasy. Hands on hips, he stood at the front of the stage and shook his head disapprovingly.

A thin man dressed in denim and wearing wire framed glasses stood and addressed the audience. Some members of the audience applauded.

"Let's take it easy," he called to the group. His appeal calmed the audience. Mike Riter, leader of the campus Socialist faction, had earned the respect of many divergent groups. He'd established a solid reputation for his considerable work in areas of social concern.

"Mr. Steers," he continued, "we're worried about the fact that since one grant for literature almost three years ago, no work from this school has been chosen for assistance. Some people think the school's been blackballed because some council members didn't like what resulted from the last award given to an OU student."

"I guess you're referring to Mr. Show's short story," Skippy answered.

"But that's not correct. Mr. Show's fiction has nothing to do with anyone's judging the works of other writers or artists."

Riter held up a piece of old newspaper. "Two years ago, you went on record as, and I quote, 'deploring the pornographic nature of the writing supported, accidentally, by the Oklahoma Council for the Arts.' Then you said that if elected Director of the Council, you would assure that no more pornography from, and I again quote, 'those nutsos in Norman will be funded by council money.' Don't you think we have reason to be worried?"

"Not if you don't write pornography!" Skippy responded.

"And how do you define pornography? You called Show's short story pornographic, and it won the O'Henry competition," Riter continued.

"He used language in his short story that appeared nowhere in the excerpts we judged."

"So language can be judged pornographic?" Riter asked.

"If used to debase, yes it can!"

"What exactly did you object to in Show's story?"

"For one thing he described women in vulgar ways."

"Judging from this newspaper clipping, the word you had trouble with was spelled c blank, blank, blank, which I assume was cunt."

Skippy's faced turned red. "There are ladies present. Please watch your language!"

"I'm not trying to insult anyone, but if some of us are writing and want to use certain words, we need to know what's acceptable and what isn't. If some words will automatically disqualify us, we want to avoid them." The audience voiced its mock approval.

"For instance is 'pussy' acceptable?" Riter continued.

"I think enough's been said on this matter, and if you continue this lewd behavior, I'll have security remove you from the hall!"

One young woman stood. "Is 'snatch' okay and how bout 'twat'?"

The audience joined in. "Can we use 'honey pot,' 'poon-tang', 'vulva', 'slippery notch', 'hair pie', 'nookey'? How bout 'vagina'?"

Another woman in the audience stood. "If we call a man's penis, 'cock', 'prick', 'dick', 'pleasure tool', 'heavy hammer', will we be disqualified?"

Skippy pounded on the lectern, but the shouting continued. He put his hands over his ears. This only encouraged the hecklers to yell louder. The other council members on stage looked outraged and nervous. They talked among themselves, shook their heads and wrung their hands. One matron stomped her foot and shook her finger at the audience.

Skippy looked as though he were close to a heart attack. "And you wonder why this campus has the sorry reputation it does! The shame!" He addressed the two women who were still standing, "How can you call yourselves women?"

In unison they shouted, "Because we have cunts, twats, honey pots...." Almost the entire audience moved towards the stage, laughing and shouting genital euphemisms. Although loud, they intended no physical harm to anyone.

The council members did not perceive the group's playfulness. They were on their feet, visibly shaken. Campus security arrived, pushed its way through the crowd, and escorted the council members out of the meeting room.

Art busily wrote down any slang terms he hadn't heard before. To assure English Department participation, he yelled, "Pudendum! Pudendum! Pudendum!" before Skippy and the others left the room.

Back at the apartment, Carl sat in the living room reading. "How'd the meeting go?"

"Not too well. Campus Security had to intervene."

"No kidding! What happened?"

"Something about Show's short story and censorship. I'm not sure. The audience got loud, and the council got bent out of shape.

He described the evening's events. Carl listened, laughing mildly, but not approvingly. "Sounds like the crazies on both sides were loose. Are you going to submit your play?"

"I'll wait till the smoke clears."

"Words," Pollard commented. "Interesting how they affect people. I guess that's part of the reason we're here."

"It's amazing. Walking home I thought about this thing tonight. I'm sitting, laughing at the reaction this jerk is having to four letter words, feeling superior because they have no affect on me. Bingo it hits me! My route to Vietnam, then back here, paved with words. Remember a guy in '61 saying, 'Ask not what your Country can do for you. Ask what you can do for your Country.' I got hooked. Now what's obscene? JFK inspired thousands to kill, die, and for what? So some yahoo from Harvard could turn the Oval Office into a whorehouse, feed his ego and pursue manifest destiny."

"Hey, take it easy," Carl offered. "You made some gigantic leaps in logic. You believe all that stuff about Kennedy?"

"It's probably true."

"But Vietnam? He wasn't even around," Carl argued.

"Look at his legacy," Art countered. "He helped rev things up, kept the Dulles boys' philosophy alive, then added his own perverse touch of inspiration for those stupid enough to believe him. For the disenfranchised, it didn't make any difference. It never has. They kill and die just like they're told to. They're the cannon fodder. The poor plus a few unlucky fucks whose draft numbers came up. But the idealist, the Pollards, the Patowskis, they're the ones he counted on to add credibility to his plan, to lead the others and convince them they weren't crazy. We were had."

"I think there are complexities that have to be factored into any conclusion about Vietnam," Carl responded. "I'm not faulting anyone who went over there."

"Me either. I just wish the hell I'd known more about what was going on."

"There are times when you do what you think is right. If the decision's a bad one, you can't destroy your entire life. You have to figure you made the best decision you could at the time based on what you knew, especially if the motivation sprang from idealism."

"Idealism? We could have a long discussion on that word," Art noted.

"I mean in the sense you went there to defend our way of life, to protect it and give people over there a chance to experience democracy."

"Even if that's bullshit?"

"Yeah, even if that's bullshit. Don't be so hard on yourself."

Art shrugged. "Maybe. I know I'm trying to make something complicated simple. Let's save it for another day over a jug of cheap wine. I need to grade papers."

"Before you start, there were two calls for you. The messages are on the note pad by the telephone. It seems your women are acting up. The one, Melanie, said she'd call tomorrow in the Grad Assistants' office after your three o'clock class."

Art's heart skipped a beat. "Did she say anything else, leave a number?"

"No, it sounded like long distance."

Without a number, he had to wait.

The second number was local, and he smiled when he heard Lauren's voice. "Hello, Arthur?"

"This is Art. Where are you?"

"I'm staying with girlfriends. Their apartment is only a few blocks from your place."

"If I'd known, we could have gotten together tonight, but it's too late now. How long you staying there?"

"The rest of the week. That's why I called. Everyone here will be out tomorrow night, and I wondered if you'd like to come for dinner?"

"Sure!"

"Good! We're in the Oakville apartments, number 111. There's a trash dumpster in the driveway closest to the apartment."

"Sounds good. I'll see you tomorrow night."

"Arthur, I mean Art, do you like seafood?"

He grabbed the list of words he'd written down at the meeting. "I love bearded clam."

"Bearded what?"

Carl overheard and laughed.

"Nothing, Lauren, just a little figurative language I picked up this evening. Seafood is great. I'll see you tomorrow." He hung up the receiver.

"She sounds young," Carl commented.

"She's nineteen."

"Aren't you a little long in the tooth for her?"

"I'm long in all the right places for her. Wait till you see her. You'll understand."

Art retired to his bedroom and spent the next four hours grading papers, though preoccupied with Melanie's call. He hadn't seen her since Orin's and wondered what had happened. No graceful way to check on her seemed possible, but he had been worried.

The next day passed like a Dali creation. Clocks melted, seconds dripped into minutes, minutes into hours. His afternoon class finally over, alone in the Grad Assistant office, the telephone rang.

"Art, is that you?" Melanie asked.

"Yes, where are you?"

"Home in Fulton. Are you okay?"

"Yes, but what are you doing there?"

"I dropped out of school. Everything came unraveled. I couldn't stay," Melanie stated.

"I don't understand. What came unraveled? You never talked to me. I had no idea you were having problems."

"I received a lot of pressure from home. But compared with what you have going on inside, it's nothing. I decided I had to come back here to face it."

"Face what?"

"It's too complicated to get into. I'm getting married the weekend after next. The guy's a doctor I've known for a long time."

"Married? Jesus! Do you know what you're doing? I know we were together only a few weeks, but…"

"It's the best thing for me," she interrupted. "You have things to work through, and I can't help with them. We were friends, and I want you to remember me that way. I need a favor too."

"What?"

"Tell Richard what I'm doing."

"Melanie, I'm not certain I want to get in the middle of that. I don't really know the guy."

"Please, just tell him what I'm doing, nothing else."

"What good will that do?"

"It will end it."

"You can't do that?"

"He won't take my calls. Please?"

Reluctantly, Art agreed. He tried to wrest more information from her, but she wouldn't say much. She made him reiterate his promise, thanked him, and said good-bye.

He arrived at the Philosophy Department as a secretary closed the office for the day.

"Excuse me, I wondered if you could tell me how to get in touch with Richard Coffer. I tried his Norman telephone, but no one answers."

"Richard's gone back to England. He left either yesterday afternoon or this morning. He came by two days ago to tell us he decided to pursue his studies at London University. He'll be sending us a forwarding address. Would you like me to send it to you?"

"No, that won't be necessary. Thank you." He chose to pursue it no further, suspecting Melanie's departure and Richard's trip were causally related.

For reasons not totally clear, knowing that she was gone hurt. Rightly or wrongly, the pain he experienced went beyond their brief relationship. It represented another failed opportunity, with no understanding of exactly why it hadn't worked out and reinforced his suspicion that he could attain nothing beyond a physical union, that the shallowness he'd used as a facade to shield himself against phantoms he couldn't define defeated more than it protected him.

Art spent the next hour and a half at O'Connell's Irish Pub. By the time he found Lauren's apartment, his considerable consumption of beer had made the world appear less gloomy. She had two bottles of chilled white wine and crab crepes waiting. He concentrated on the wine.

Carl had not expected to hear from Art that evening and was surprised when Lauren, crying, telephoned and asked for his help.

"Please, you have to come here. Arthur won't listen to me. He's gone crazy!"

"What's he done?"

"Please come over," she pleaded. "I need your help."

In a few minutes, he knocked on her door. "Where's Art?" Carl asked.

She led him outside to the trash dumpster. "He's in there. Before I called you, he said he's not fit to live with other human beings, but knew where he belonged. When he started to leave, I begged him to stay and not drive. He said he wasn't driving, then left. I watched him walk over here and climb into the dumpster. I begged him to come out, but he told me to leave him alone."

"Got a flashlight?" Carl asked Lauren.

She ran back into the apartment and returned with one. Carl turned it on and opened the dumpster door. There, in the middle of bags of garbage, soiled newspapers and discarded boxes, Art, spread-eagle, clutched what remained of a bottle of wine.

"Are you planning on spending the night here?" Carl asked.

"The rest of my life."

"Your rent's paid for this month."

"This is where I belong, in the trash bin of history," Art slurred.

Carl laughed. "I don't think this qualifies as such a lofty abode. Besides, where will the English Department send your check?"

"Fuck the English Department."

"I suppose the same applies to your G.I. Bill check?"

"No, double-fuck the government!"

"Okay, fine." Carl closed the door and turned to leave. Lauren's desperate look made him try again.

He trained the flashlight's beam directly into Art's eyes. "Tomorrow morning when the garbage truck comes, they'll pick this thing up and you and all this garbage will go through a shredder. I don't know how long you'll be conscious, but it won't be pleasant."

Art shielded his eyes from the beam as much as possible. "A kind of

Patowski coleslaw with a little garbage dressing," he mumbled.

"That's right," Carl laughed.

"Shit!" Art took the last swig of his wine, stood as best he could, and climbed out. Carl offered his hand to help. "Damn, you smell!"

Art curtsied. "No sir! You smell; I stink!"

Carl drove Art and his car back to the duplex. Lauren followed in Carl's car. While he drove her back, Art took a cold shower.

When Carl returned he offered to take Art's classes the next day.

"No need. The shower helped, and with some sleep I'll be 100 percent. I never miss classes, at least not because of partying or other self-indulgences. A little Cotton Mather inside me screams, 'Work! Work!' I'll be fine, but thanks."

"No problem. See ya in the morning."

The next day, head cleared, Art resolved to end the relationship with Lauren. Although he thought the question of propriety remained moot, he knew the appearance of impropriety was irrefutable. His performance at her dinner party clearly indicated the inner turmoil with which he continued to wrestle. Art knew Lauren's youth did not supply her with the tools she needed to deal with his problems. The idea of him as an intellectual mentor had limited merit. The idea of him as an emotional mentor had none. At this moment and place in time, he could only take from any relationship. He had nothing to give.

Although they saw each other in class, he decided to wait until Saturday to talk with her. If he'd allowed himself to look at her in class, if he'd honestly evaluated himself and his motivations, he would have admitted how little chance existed of his walking away from her. But he didn't allow his eyes to dwell on her loveliness, nor his conscience to dwell on his intentions.

Saturday afternoon, overnight case in hand, she arrived, her youth radiating a beauty distinct from physical presence. He felt his small resolve dissolve like a vapor.

"Hey sailor," she called as she walked in the front door. "You doing anything tonight?" She put her arms around his neck and kissed him. Her knee went gently into his groin. He tried, but not too hard, to separate her hands from behind his neck. As their kiss continued, his excitement rose above his intent. He lifted the bottom of her sweater above her breasts. She released him and raised her arms so he could remove it altogether. He bent and suckled each breast, rolling the tip of his tongue around her pink nipples, in full bloom. Breathing hard, she pulled back and walked to the sofa, sliding off her jeans and underwear.

Art pulled the ottoman to them. She slid down to assure her back and head were supported by the sofa, while her butt rested on the ottoman. He kissed her breasts and stomach, then proceeded to feast on her pussy, concentrating on her special spot, but taking time to enter her with his tongue, penetrating as deeply as possible. Her sighs and moans increased. As he licked and probed, he raised his eyes to watch her fondle her breasts, raising them to her outstretched tongue, quivering each time its tip found a nipple. When she came, her intensity lifted her off of the ottoman. Art recovered in time to catch her lovely bottom before it hit the floor. He placed her back on the ottoman, entered her, stroked three or four times, then pulled out and straddled her. He placed his still wet face between the inside of her breasts to moisten them, then put his penis between her breasts, held them firmly, and started an up and down motion. When her breasts grew dry, he repeated the process.

When their throbbing stopped, he held her and savored her smell until the late Saturday afternoon shadows slipped into the edge of darkness.

As they dressed, he felt fatigue from their indulgence and his lack of resolution.

Art drove to McGaw's, who'd invited them for a beer to celebrate his completion of the qualifying exam. When they arrived, another couple, Gary and Lydia Garnett, were leaving. They'd stopped by Matt's and Virginia's to announce their last weekend as man and wife.

"Yes," Gary started, "Monday the divorce is final. She'll be rid of me legally for good."

"Congratulations, I guess," Art offered.

"We're trying to be civilized about the whole thing. Are you two married?" Gary asked.

"No."

Gary looked at Lauren approvingly. "Next week I'm a free man."

She blushed and laughed. Lydia grabbed his arm. "That's next week, not tonight."

After Gary and Lydia left, Matt explained the situation. "I've never seen two people split up on such friendly terms. But Gary's getting into some pretty weird stuff," Matt explained. "They have two great kids, and Lydia's worried that something will happen to them. She loves him, but if he insists on doing all the crap he wants to, she doesn't want the kids around it."

"What's he doing?"

"He wants to find out which of society's rules he needs, which he doesn't," Matt answered. "Gary wants to test them all. Last month he drove to California to sleep with his sister. When he sprung the program on his sister, her husband went ape shit, threw him out of the house. On the trip out there and back he ran up more than $10,000 in credit card bills with no intention of paying them."

"I guess I'm obtuse," Art stated. "Anyone with a brain can see the world isn't safe for anarchy."

"He feels he has to test the limits," Matt responded. "He wanted me to drive with him to Houston next week. He plans to raise hell down there, do acid all the way. I told him I just finished the qualifying exam and didn't think the English Department would appreciate my taking a sabbatical two months after I started teaching. Gary laughed, said I'm a slave to the system."

Art shrugged. "Aren't we all? Even Gary. But how did your exam go?"

"Pretty well. I think..." Matt jumped to his feet. "Shit!" He ran to the bookcase. Fred the cat leaped away to avoid Matt's wrath. "Fucking cat is always getting into my marijuana!"

"I imagine it's tough for him to score a lid."

Matt didn't see the humor. "I can't stand that bastard." He sat and started to roll a joint, telling Art how he'd approached the exam.

"I told them what I thought about whatever the subject was, gave them examples of my ideas. Generally, I feel good about the test. We'll see. I could have waited to take it, but what the hell. I didn't want my masters riding on it next semester. That would be too much pressure."

They discussed Art's upcoming exams for the MA and his study approach. After an hour and a few beers, he and Lauren left for a movie.

In the theater, his lust momentarily quelled, his conscience started to haunt him. He decided Matt had suggested the perfect out with Lauren, studying for his Master exams.

Back at the apartment, Art brought up his concerns. "I'm afraid we're not going to be able to see each other as much as we have. I have to get ready for my exams."

"We can study together," she responded.

"That doesn't seem to work. I get distracted." She laughed. He didn't. "Lauren, I can't mess up these exams. I have to pass."

"You will. We'll work out something," she said, snuggling into his arms.

Throughout the weekend, Art continued to plant the seeds of their separation.

The following week proved uneventful until Thursday night. When he returned to the apartment after six hours in the library, Carl nearly ran him down rushing to his car. When in the car, he explained the crisis.

"Red Dick and his wife called. Virginia is with them. They got the results of the qualifying exam. Matt and Red Dick only made it through the MA. Matt went bull shit. Started drinking, smoking dope. Then he began breaking things, throwing stuff around the apartment. He went after Virginia and the cat. She managed to get out and went to Red Dick's."

"Doesn't he know he gets another shot next semester?"

Carl shrugged. "Who knows."

"How's Red Dick doing?" Art asked.

"He's philosophical about it. This was his second time. He's now a terminal MA."

"Sounds like a sickness," Art said, shaking his head in disappointment and disgust.

At Matt's apartment, lights shone, music blared. Matt, thoroughly drunk and loaded, let them in. Furniture had been upended, books were scattered everywhere, broken glass from pictures and bottles littered the floor. "Lava King," Art commented, "this place looks like Saigon in '68."

"Maid's night out," Matt slurred. He started to lose his balance, but Art caught him before he went down. Carl righted the sofa and helped seat Matt. The arm on the stereo had been set to continually replay the Nitty Gritty Dirt Band's version of "Mr. Bojangles."

"You guys wanna beer?" Matt asked. "Don't mind if I do," Carl responded. Matt tried to get up. "I'll get them," Carl offered. "Where's Fred?" he asked.

"I don't know, but when I find him the world will be minus one feline," Matt mumbled, almost falling over onto one side. "I have to go to the bathroom." Carl helped him stand.

When he closed the bathroom door, Carl walked to the stereo and stopped the music. "I can't listen to that again."

"At least he didn't get the cat."

"Right," Carl responded. "I think we can safely report that Fred's all right, wherever he is."

They heard Matt flush the toilet and waited for his return. Instead, they heard the toilet handle clang repeatedly. There were pauses, then the clanging started again. Carl looked at Art puzzled.

"What the hell's he doing?"

"We'd better check."

Art knocked on the bathroom door. "Matt, is everything okay?" All they could hear were blurred obscenities and his attempts to flush the toilet. Art opened the door.

Matt stood on the closed toilet seat, bending to flush and re-flush, cursing incoherently.

Art approached him. "Hey guy, what's going on?" Matt whirled, his elbow aimed full tilt at Art's nose. He turned quickly to avoid a broken beak, but the blow landed squarely against Art's right temple and drove him into the bathroom wall.

The swing caused Matt to lose his balance, and Carl grabbed him around the waist and lifted him off the toilet. He held Matt a few feet above the floor, clear of his thrashing arms and fists.

"Are you okay?" Carl managed to ask Art.

"Yeah, he hit me in my least vulnerable spot."

On a hunch, Art lifted the toilet seat. There, spread-eagle, eyes wide as silver dollars, tail bushed, Fred the cat clung to the slippery porcelain bowl for dear life. Upon seeing light and Art's face, he let out a scream of fear, anger, and outrage, then leaped from the toilet past all the crazy humans and retreated to the safety of his secret hiding place.

Matt, exhausted by his efforts, slumped in Carl's grasp. They put him to bed, filled Fred's food bowl, and left. Back at their apartment, Carl and Art called Rouge and talked to Virginia. With Carl's assurance of Fred's safety, she agreed to spend the night with Red Dick and Darlene.

CHAPTER NINE

Art held firm to his study schedule and encouraged Lauren to date.

Before their relationship started, Lauren's philosophy professor, Max Hanna, had eagerly sought her affections. An authority on Rationalism, he held a special love for Hedonism. When Art won Lauren's favors, Max did not take the loss well.

One evening shortly after Art and Lauren had started their version of the beast with two backs, Art and Matt had stopped at the Library Bar for a beer. Max and a few friends were playing pool. As Art passed the pool table, Max swung his elbow into Art's shoulder.

"You have a problem?" Max asked menacingly.

"Just you, dick-head," Art retorted angrily. Art noted Max's left shoulder rise slightly and acted before he could use the pool cue as a weapon. He grabbed Max's shirt collar with both hands, pushed him hard back onto the pool table and solidly punched him with a right uppercut to the jaw. Dazed by the blow, Max offered little resistance.

Matt stepped in front of one of Max's friends who started to intervene. "This is between the two of them," Matt warned. The young man backed away.

"Shit, man! Give it a rest!" Max yelled, raising his hands to protect his face.

"No more shit, asshole!" Art growled with anger and conviction. He loosened his grip and stepped back, ready for more action. Max, who had expected a war of words, got off the pool table and hurried from the bar, slamming the door behind him.

Thus, Art was not pleased when he learned of Lauren's decision to date Max, but given the circumstances, he could say little. His feelings about Max came from more than their brief skirmish. Art sensed some darkness of soul that Max worked to hide.

Both men were the same age, their only similarity. An Associate Professor, Max measured a thin six feet tall. He wore sandals, and his shoulder-length, scraggly, dirty looking brown hair hung past his shoulders. His dark, brown eyes appeared sorrowful, even when he laughed. Max reminded Art of Jesus with a hangover.

One Saturday night at Art's apartment after Lauren's second date with Max, Art's curiosity overtook his better sense.
"How'd it go last night?" he asked.
"Fine, but I thought we weren't going to ask each other about our dates."
"I haven't had one."
"Tell me if you don't want me to see anyone else."
"That wouldn't be fair. I'm just curious. What's it like dating a philosopher? Do you feel wiser?"
"He's nice, quiet, kind of shy. Gary Garnett's a friend of his. We saw him at a party last night."
"How'd he behave?"
"Fair. He was loaded, but other than making a lunge for me, he was fine."
"Lunge?"
"He was sitting on the floor and said something I couldn't hear. When I bent over, he tried to pull me down. He'd dropped acid."
"Sounds like an interesting crowd."
"There were a lot of drugs, especially LSD and cocaine. Have you tried either?"
"I limit my vices to those I can afford." He took a long swallow of his open beer.
"I hope it's not too tame, but tonight you'll get drunk like the good Lord intended."

When the telephone rang, he asked Lauren to answer it. She spoke guardedly for a minute, then returned to him.
"Socrates?" he asked.
"If you mean Max, yes," she answered awkwardly.
"What's up?"
"He wants to see me."
Art shrugged. "So?"
"He said he'd come for me, if I wanted."
"Well?"

"I'm not sure."

"What's not to be sure about. You had something in mind when you told him you'd be here tonight." Art could not disguise his irritation.

"What do you think, Arthur?"

"I think I'm tired of the name Arthur. Call and tell him to pick you up."

She gazed at the floor. He went to her and gently turned her face to him. "You obviously want to go. I won't tell you not to."

"All right," she replied softly, looking away.

He brought the telephone to her. "Have him wait about half an hour," he said as he took her in his arms.

She pulled back. "I can't. I wouldn't feel anything."

"That quickly!"

"If you wanted me to stay, it would be different! You don't care!"

"You should be here only if you want to be here, with no promises," he responded.

"What should I do?" she pleaded.

"Call him."

She telephoned Max, then collected her things. After opening the door, she looked back at him: "Will this affect my grade?"

Art shook his head in disbelief, put down the book he'd pretended to be reading, and pointed to the street. "Leave!"

Unable to focus, he did nothing until he heard Max's car arrive and the quick sound of a door opening and closing. Any image of her in his mind's eye would destroy his resolve. He'd looked forward to the sex, but this was a way to end it with her actively involved in the decision. A bruised ego and aching loins were small prices to pay. "Zero for two," he murmured out loud.

That night, he could not work. He drank two six-packs and fell asleep in the living room watching the late night movie.

Sunday, he channeled his energy towards his studies. The extra time with the books would help him through the Masters examinations, now less than three weeks away.

Extra work also helped keep Lauren out of his mind, although seeing her two mornings during the week proved difficult. She sat in the back of the room, avoided eye contact, and departed as soon as class ended.

Each afternoon, he went to the library, all spare time devoted to preparation for the approaching exams. This concentration kept his lust and anxiety in check.

On those evenings when he returned to the apartment before Carl had turned in, they discussed English Department politics, women and sometimes, Vietnam, although Nam remained a delicate area for both men.

Some of their time in-Country had overlapped. Carl had been a platoon leader in I Corps and had engaged in some of the worst fighting of the war. Art had spent most of his time in Saigon, venturing into the bush only half a dozen times. Those sorties and his fighting during Tet gave him some understanding of Carl's experience, but the realization that Carl had faced that level of intensity for most of his tour made Art self-conscious about discussing his experiences and reactions.

He could quantify the difference between their experiences: Art knew the whistling sound bullets make as they pass a man's head. He'd heard them many times during Tet, but he'd returned without a scratch. Carl carried so much VC shrapnel in his body he couldn't pass through an airport security point without setting off its metal detector.

Trust developed with their talks. Both recognized their limited access. No one else in the immediate vicinity could understand what they had witnessed, had done. Rob De Clines had held a rear echelon position and hadn't fought. None of their other friends had served. As Commander of the Reserve unit, Carl couldn't share personal revelations with his subordinates.

One evening, Art took a respite from his studies and consumed a large quantity of Gallo's Pink Chablis. Carl went through a six pack of Bud. The television's ten o'clock news reported a bad day of fighting in Nam. They watched the battle scenes in silence. When the report ended, Art spoke first.

"I couldn't get past the fear. I'd never been so fucking afraid in my life. The only way I did anything was on sheer instinct. In the middle of any of it, I couldn't think at all. When the fighting stopped, the fear returned. I felt so ashamed of my fear."

"You'd been an idiot not to be afraid."

"On the south side of Chicago, you didn't admit fear. If you felt it, you kept quiet." He hesitated, "You were afraid too?"

"Hell yes," Carl laughed. "Anyone not afraid had to be nuts. You didn't hear anything, because everyone assumed it was universal. Sure, I felt it, but the fear doesn't haunt me, it's the men I led into that stinking jungle. I can't forget them. Like ghosts, they're always there, some worse than others.

"I had a Lance Corporal from Iowa. The kid loved me like a father. We'd arrived in-Country the same day. For seven months, we were together on every patrol I led into the bush in Quang Tri, a real bitch. There were close calls; a lot of guys died, but we both made it as though our lives were charmed. Guys next to us had their heads blown off, but we were fine.

"Then it happened. Our turn. We'd been out of base camp an hour. He was point, about twenty yards ahead of us. I didn't see it, but he stepped on a claymore mine. We heard the explosion, everything blurred. We groped for cover, but land mines were everywhere. When the mines stopped, the VC started. It was a perfect ambush. Those still alive, dug in and returned fire. We could hear the kid screaming. I'd taken six or seven hits and bled like a stuck pig. Two of the guys went to get him. They made it back, dragging him, both his legs gone. He begged me to kill him, to blow his brains out. He cried, screamed, grabbed at my 45."

"Christ! did you?"

Carl looked at him puzzled. "No! I put tourniquets on what was left of his legs, got some morphine into him and concentrated on fighting the gooks to keep the rest of us alive."

"You never considered killing him?"

"No."

"That's the difference between us. I would have."

"You wouldn't have killed him. I've been around you enough to know that," Carl responded.

"But I would have considered it. That's why you're a leader of men. Early on over there, I got too wrapped up internally to feel confident about right or wrong. As crazy as the war looked, I couldn't get past the obligation and responsibilities I'd signed up for. Thinking, decisions, they're enough to drive anyone nuts.

"Yesterday, I read a Yeats poem I hadn't seen, 'Adam's Curse.' An underlying idea is that because of Adam's fall, man must earn his bread by the sweat from his brow. I'm not certain I agree. The curse might be thinking, consciousness. A dog doesn't debate morality."

"Would you really prefer that level of existence?"

Art waited a moment, but could not surrender to the wine and emotion. "No," he conceded. "Actually, it might be the exact opposite. Consciousness may be our potential salvation, the route to something more substantial than this absurd world of chance. I'm not sure. But I do know the edge is what we have. Halfway between the beasts and the heavens. It's a hell of a position. It creates situations like having to make the decision you did about the kid."

"I had no choice," Carl stated. "You wouldn't have had one. In combat, you said you operated on instincts. They would have stopped you from killing him."

"I don't know," Art said as he took a long swallow of wine. "It's all like a distant nightmare."

"Speaking of which, a few nights ago I heard you having a bad one. It sounded like you couldn't breath. By the time I got to your door, you'd quieted down so I didn't bother you."

"It's always the same. I'm back in the jungle. You ever have that problem?"

"As I said, it's the waking dreams that get to me. Are you all right?" Carl asked.

"I think so, guess it's part of the healing process. I'll probably have worse nightmares after the Masters exams."

"Are you ready?"

"I wish I knew what to expect," Art responded. "Professors Manly and Dells are two of the graders, and I'm taking their classes."

"Concentrate on their questions, which you should recognize, and feed them back their ideas," Carl suggested.

"You're kidding? Earlier this semester I railed against the shit Manly throws out in class and warned a kid about taking it too seriously. You'd think they'd be interested in new ideas," Art stated.

"Don't be a hero. The exam consists of four essay questions. You should have three locked by the classes you're taking. What's your other class?"

"Victorian Poetry from Candless."

"Good, he usually grades them. Any Victorian questions should be his. I'll take your classes the Monday and Tuesday you're testing," Carl offered.

"That will help. Say hello to Lauren for me."

"What happened to her?"

Carl looked relieved as Art related the story.

"I didn't think you'd been seeing her the past week or so. It's probably a good thing. She is your student," Carl reminded him.

"I know; she's just so damn gorgeous and ready to please."

"There's plenty of that around. It wouldn't hurt to scout for a more appropriate screwing partner, someone like your buddy Judith Hunter, who I saw today in Kaufmann. In fact, she asked about you."

"What's the story with her?"

"I think she's married to a grad student in the Poly Sci Department, but I get the impression she's looking for some action."

"A fine looking lady. Any kids?"

"I don't think so. Check it out," Carl suggested.

"All I need is a jealous husband taking a shot at me. If you think she's after extracurricular activity, why haven't you stepped in?"

"For the record, you wretched shitbird, I'm serious about Clare. Don't fall in love. Just get your wick wet. I told Judith you're preparing for the Masters exams and spending a lot of time in the library. She said she might drop by to see you. Since I thought Teeny Bopper had gone to greener pastures, I figured you might be interested."

"Bullwinkle! I'm touched at your concern. Speaking of Clare, are you two going to do the thing?"

"What thing?"

"You know, marriage, the pitter patter of little moose hoofs running around the house," Art responded laughing.

"I have no plans and nothing's going to happen till I'm finished with this crap. By the way, you'll meet her at Cunning's on Thanksgiving."

"Great! If you want her to stay here, I can bunk elsewhere."

"She's staying with De Clines. Thanks though, I might take you up on that in the future."

"No problem, just let me know. Think I'll turn in now, and thanks for the lead on Judith. I'll sleep on it."

The next evening in the library, Art could not hide his pleasure at Judith's finding him.

"Carl told me you were spending your evenings here," she whispered.

He rose and motioned her to follow him to the foyer where they could talk without disturbing anyone.

"It's good to see you."

"I'm checking up on you for Demetrius. Every time I mention your name, he gets this dreamy look in his eyes."

"Great, a weird dog loves me. Now if his owner got that look, I'd feel as though I'd accomplished something."

Judith smiled. "Maybe she does. Why don't you stop by my office. We can get a cup of coffee."

"See you tomorrow," he answered, delighted.

With lecherous anticipation, he watched her walk away. Only a brain dead eunuch could misinterpret her smile and body language.

Judith shared an office with Kay Whitehall, who Art knew from their Yeats seminar.

"Hi, how are you?" she offered.

"Great, I didn't know you and Judith officed together."

"I didn't know you two knew each other."

"Her dog and I go back a long way. Now Judith and I are working on a project together," he stated.

"What's that?" Kay asked.

"Possible affects of anachronisms in literature."

"Like what?"

Judith rolled her chair out from behind her desk. "Yes, I'd like to hear about this myself." She wore a leather miniskirt that started his blood boiling.

"Well, for instance, what would be the literary implications of Hester Prynne having the pill or Moby Dick being an endangered species?"

"I get the idea," Kay said, grinning and turning to gather her papers and books.

He appreciated Judith's crossing her legs and the glimpse of her sheer lace panties. Knowing, however, the physical reaction he would quickly manifest, he concentrated on Kay. "Do you have to leave?"

"Yes, but sometime in the next week or two, I'd like to talk with you about your paper in the seminar."

"Sure, wait until after the masters exams. I'm about halfway through my paper, but won't finish until the exams are over."

"God, halfway through! I haven't even started. We'll talk later."

After she left, he walked to Judith and stood in front of her. She remained seated, but shifted her glance from his face to the bulge that had started in his pants.

"It's good to see you. I hoped you'd show. It looks like your happy to see me, or is that a magic marker in your jeans?"

"Maybe a magic wand. We'll find out."

He closed the window blinds, then locked the office door.

He returned to her, leaned forward and kissed her. She responded, putting her arms around his neck.

"The pressures of studying for the exams, teaching and keeping up with classes are taking a toll," he said as he ran his hands through her hair. "I need some relief."

"Where's your young friend?"

"I'm not seeing her any more."

She rubbed his penis through his pants. "Good."

They kissed again, long and hard. With her help, he unzipped his pants and freed his hard cock. Without looking up she said, "Relief is just a swallow away," then filled her mouth with him, sucking and licking to please him and herself.

He lifted her sweater so he could suck her small breasts. Her leather skirt went to her waist, enabling him to lower her panties. He felt crazed with lust and wanted to experience her in every way possible. They made love on her desk, soiling some of the Freshman themes she'd been grading and knocking them to the floor.

He delighted in her uninhibited joy. Despite the discomfort, she performed with passionate enthusiasm. With his happiness at being inside of her, a desk of nails wouldn't have bothered him. He climaxed quickly.

"Excuse the hurry. It's been almost three weeks."

"You were great," she responded. They heard the office door next to them open. "That's the janitor," she cautioned. "He comes by every day at this time."

"The Jesus freak?"

"Yes."

"Too bad he didn't wander in a few minutes ago. He would've had some real material for his campus corner ministry. Let's get a cup of coffee and come back later," Art recommended. She dressed and picked up the spotted papers they'd knocked on the floor.

"Tell your students you spilled coffee on them."

"Glue," she laughed.

They walked to the closest campus dorm cafeteria, which had started to fill with students for the dinner meal, and found a secluded spot.

"Damn! The stuff they're eating smells as bad as it looks," he commented.

"Is it as bad as the Army's?"

"Probably. How'd you know I'd been in the Army?"

"Carl told me, but with your fatigue jacket, it doesn't take Dick Tracy."

"You and Carl talk a lot."

"Not as much as I would have liked."

"You mean he was numero uno on the hit parade, or should I say fuck parade? That makes me feel good."

"Don't let your ego go crazy. I've been looking for someone, and Carl was a candidate. But from talking to him, I knew we couldn't get together. After today, I'm not disappointed."

"Did you get interested in me with the lakeside incident?"

She laughed. "Before that. I'd seen you around the department. I thought you were looking at me."

"You're an attractive, sexy lady. I can't believe you'd have any difficulty finding male companionship."

"I don't want any male companion."

"Not to be indelicate, but Carl thought you were married."

"For the third time," she responded

"Third time!"

"I married in high school when I was sixteen. It lasted less than a year, created a small scandal in Muskogee, my home town."

"You're the Okie from Muskogee?"

"One of them. When I was an undergraduate here, I married a football player. We divorced my senior year."

"What happened?"

"He caught me in the act with an assistant coach."

"That will do it. Am I going to be a surrogate for the coach?"

"No; this is different. My husband, Larry, is a great guy. He's smart, funny, sensitive and really loves me. We've been together almost two years."

"What's the problem?"

"He's impotent. It started over six months ago. Nothing I or anyone else does turns him on."

"If you can't I recommend putting a mirror under his nose."

"He's going to a psychologist, but so far nothing has helped. We've tried other women he liked who were willing, even prostitutes. He knows I need release. As long as we don't rub his nose in what we're doing, there won't be trouble. I don't want to hurt Larry, but celibacy wasn't part of the agreement. It had been six months for me. You don't know how great that felt in the office." She reached across the table and touched his hands.

"Yes I do. What's your time situation?" he asked.

"Whatever is available during the day, some evenings when he's studying, and an occasional weekend day."

"Fine. Right now my schedule's hectic. I have the exams in two weeks; I'm teaching six hours and taking three classes. We'll have to coordinate schedules. Is that acceptable?"

"Yes," she smiled.

"Once I've completed the exams, my schedule will be more manageable." He finished his coffee. "Let's go back to your office. The holy roller should be finished. I have some time before I need to hit the books."

In the office, he proceeded carefully, assuring her pleasure, withdrawing when he felt himself close and using his tongue until he could re-enter her without fear of ejaculation. They continued until she had to leave for home and he for the library. That evening, he had difficulty thinking about anything but her.

Judith brought a new dimension of excitement to Art's world. Each day remaining before Thanksgiving break, he met with her for as long as their schedules permitted, devoting most of their time to sex, each taking pleasure from the other without inhibition or concern, exhausting every copulation position either knew or had heard of, including a few yoga positions that proved challenging.

He thought he'd found the perfect fucking machine. She stood 5'4" to his 5' 9", one hundred evenly distributed pounds to his one hundred seventy not so evenly distributed pounds. The compatibility amazed him. She proved incredibly flexible and possessed a derriere as luscious as Lauren's but more effective because she knew how to exploit it successfully. Enthusiasm, a natural propensity, and much practice explained her ability.

"You're amazing," he commented after one of their afternoon sessions. "I get the impression you have three states of being: about to fuck, fucking or just been fucked. Then it starts all over again, the Huntian intercourse dialectic. After this time with you, I'm surprised you lasted six months without sex."

"It's my longest abstinence in a long time, but I hoped Larry would recover, and we could get on with our life. I'm not a nut on marital fidelity, but after my second marriage, I thought I'd give it a try."

"That was the football coach you were caught with?"

"He was O.U.'s first black coach."

Art laughed. "I guess you showed him how liberal Oklahomans can be." He took her hands in his. "You've talked too much today and need to be reminded of certain rules of discipline. Moreover, some of the behavior I've heard about can't go unpunished. This will hurt me more than it hurts you."

She smiled, stood, kicked off her shoes and lay across his knees.

That evening Art stayed until the library closed for the holiday. He went to De Clines' house, met Sugar, Rob's wife, Darlene, Rick's wife, and Clare. They invited him to stay for dessert and drinks.

Each woman reacted differently to him. Art troubled Sugar, as did anything outside her idea of how the world should be. She based her concern on what the men said about his relationship with Lauren. Darlene hated him instantaneously, a primal response based upon questions of propriety and decorum. She saw him as an anarchist, threatening the foundations of civilization. Clare liked him as quickly as Darlene hated him. Carl had told her about their conversations. Thus, she had some insights into Art's true thoughts and could see past the rough humor and ostensible insensitivity. With or without Carl's perceptions, she enjoyed Art's playfulness and recognized his professed male chauvinism hid a love of women in all their varied forms and hues.

Her physical beauty radiated from within, from a spirituality which glowed outward through her large, black star sapphire eyes. Her voluptuous figure, full and firm, kept Carl a happy Marine. When they were all seated at the table, Art looked directly at her but addressed Carl. "Aren't you afraid she'll regain consciousness and leave?"

"Dip shit," Carl managed. Clare smiled at Art and winked.

He stared at her large, firm breasts. "Carl said you're a paralegal. Now I know what they mean by para."

Clare tilted her head, "Art...." with a long "A" in her best Texas accent. The men howled.

"I'm only joking," he said, looking at her for forgiveness.

Carl stood with a glass of wine in hand. "We were going to do this tomorrow, but now is as good a time as any. All of us have nicknames, and we've tried to decide on one for this miserable, wretched excuse for a human being, Art, pollack, Patowski. After much careful deliberation, we've decided the 'evil gnome' is perfect, especially when one considers that a gnome is an ageless, deformed dwarf who lives in the earth or under a bridge."

He raised his glass. Rob and Rick stood with glasses held high, toasting Art, seated with the ladies, who also raised their glasses to him. "To the evil gnome," Carl continued. "May his deformity be a small one." They drank, applauded, and called for a speech from the newly-anointed.

Art stood, holding his glass high. "I'm short by some standards, but I am taller than most gnomes. What's more, my deformity doesn't show when I'm dressed. For a quarter, I'll show it in the back room to any of the ladies. At any rate, despite all these anomalies, I accept this dubious honor and hope I can live up to my new name."

He remained on his best behavior for the next hour, then left, looking forward to tomorrow and spending Thanksgiving with them at the Cunning household.

Thanksgiving Day arrived warm and clear. At Cunning's home, the balmy weather allowed the children to play in the backyard and left the living room for the adults.

Brad's wife, Marilyn, ran everything from the kitchen. A Midwesterner, she managed without any effort or need to control. Art recognized Cunning's good fortune and took every opportunity to remind him that he'd married above his station. Despite his beady eyes and the perpetual drop of sweat hanging from his lower lip, he'd found a jewel who loved him and added much to his existence.

The day reminded Art of good memories from his childhood. His mother had managed to keep Thanksgiving free from problems that accompanied most family get-togethers. His father, and later his mother's second husband, remained relatively calm, no one got drunk or fought, plates overflowed with tasty food, and events went as he dreamed.

The aromas from Marilyn's kitchen and the noise from children inside and outside the house blended perfectly with his memories. The women scurried to and fro, happy in their work. The children scampered and chattered, earnest in their play.

By half-time of the televised football game, the men sat in the living room eating the traditional Thanksgiving meal. One of the children raced through the living room pursued by another. The lead child tripped over Carl's foot, hit the floor hard and started to cry. Carl quickly reached down, picked up the boy and held him in his arms. The child roared, more frightened than injured. Carl patted his back, trying to comfort him.

His mother emerged from the kitchen, mouth and eyes wide with fear. She grabbed her son from Carl's arms.

"Leave him alone, you baby-killer!"

Art gasped. Brad exclaimed, "Jesus!" The woman's husband, a dopey-looking perennial graduate student, headed for the next room. Carl remained seated, his face frozen in bewilderment. Art started from his chair, but stopped before he stood. His eyes met Clare's. Standing in the kitchen entrance to the living room, she mirrored the pain and confusion in Carl's expression.

Clutching her son, the woman retreated to a back bedroom. Art fell back into his chair.

"I don't know what that was about," Brad said to Carl, "but you could use another beer." Carl shrugged his shoulders and walked with him into the kitchen.

Art waited a few minutes, then followed. Saying nothing, he filled his plate and opened four bottles of beer. Art took his plate and bottles into one of Cunning's two bathrooms, locked the door and proceeded to eat and drink. Art remained there over an hour, ignoring the people who knocked or sending them to the other bathroom. He emerged only after he'd finished the last of his beer.

Everything in the living room seemed normal. The men, sans the battered child's father, had returned, all silent, concentrating on whatever game was in progress. Art flashed a middle finger at Carl, which he ignored, and went to the kitchen, where most of the women talked and washed dishes.

"Can I have another beer?" Art asked. "Only if you'll dry," Marilyn answered. "I would be pleased to," he responded.

Marilyn handed an open beer and a dish towel to him. Clare had her back to him while she washed dishes in the sink.

"I can't think of more pleasant company to work with," he said as he stood beside her to begin drying. She turned and smiled. "This is sweet of you."

"I'm a pretty sweet guy. Didn't Bullwinkle tell you?"

"He said you were a little goofy."

"Just a little? He must have been in a good mood. Where did Calamity Jane and her dork husband go?"

All the women but Clare and Marilyn looked at him with shocked expressions, then looked around to see who stood near. Clare smiled. Marilyn responded, "I think they're outside with the kids."

"Is Carl all right?" he asked Clare.

"He's fine," she responded. Then under her breath added, "He's been better."

While they did the dishes, Art learned about Clare, how she had settled in Tulsa after growing up in Houston. A summary of his history followed. Intermingled were jokes and laughter. Art forgot about the incident with Carl until a large hand wrapped around his neck. "How are you, Arthur?" Carl yelled in his ear.

Art pulled away from him. "Jesus Christ! You almost broke my ear drum! Protect me from this big bully." He ran to Clare's embrace.

"You miserable, wretched beast. You shouldn't be allowed around decent people!" Carl bellowed, moving close to grab Art.

Clare, laughing, got between them. "Leave him alone. You don't know how sensitive he is."

"Sensitive?" Carl's eyes rolled back into his head.

"That's right," Art beamed. "I'm so sensitive I cry when I hear a car engine die."

Matt came into the kitchen laughing. "Hey, the hysterical broad's kid just split his lip. It looks like it's going to need stitches. She can't blame this one on Pollard."

Marilyn grabbed some bath towels on her way to the backyard. Art watched with Clare and Carl from the kitchen window as the boy and his parents left for the hospital. Marilyn rejoined the group in the kitchen.

"He'll need four or five stitches to close his lip." She shrugged her shoulders in resigned acceptance. "He climbed our fence, with his parents watching, and got into that rough place behind the yard. We warned everyone not to let their kids go outside the backyard."

"It's the gods getting even for his mother's big mouth," Art suggested. "Remember, the sins of the mother will be visited upon the heads of the son, or something like that."

"I think you got the wrong parent," Carl corrected.

"No, my friend, the kid got the wrong parent."

The accident presented a kind of perverse vindication. The remainder of the day went harmoniously, Matt's intoxication being the only circumstance to unsettle frayed sensibilities. But though drunk, Matt was happy. He played in the backyard with the remaining children and with Brad's hapless hound Grendel. Virginia gave Matt plenty of room, but watched all his activities, lurking in the shadows like a noiseless, patient spider. Before the sun disappeared, Matt passed out on the ground in the backyard with both of Brad's boys sitting on his chest and Grendel smelling his crotch.

Dale and Scott came running into the house looking for Brad. "Daddy, Daddy Mr. McGaw's dead, Mr. McGaw's dead!"

Virginia, right behind them, assured everyone that Matt was fine. Brad and Carl helped her get him into his car. Shortly after their departure, the Rouges and DeClines left. Carl pulled Art to one side.

"Would you mind staying away from the place for a couple of hours. Clare and I are going back there to get reacquainted."

"Of course not, you miserable shitbird," Art generously replied. "Do you need any help?"

"Thank you, I don't think so."

"I'm sure Brad won't mind my hanging around for awhile. I can help cleanup."

After Carl and Clare left, Brad and Art started with the backyard. When they returned to the house, Marilyn prepared her little guys for bed. Connell, their infant daughter, started crying for her evening meal. Brad put a bottle on the stove while Art watched.

"So you have the masters exams next week."

"Yeah, can't wait to get them over."

"You ready?"

"I think so. I've been going after it for about four weeks, plus I'm taking classes from two, maybe three of the graders. This break has been nice. I'm taking tomorrow off, then I'll cram on Saturday and Sunday."

"I took my MA from Kansas State. The exams were nothing as long as you passed your thesis."

"That's the trouble with a no thesis program like this. You're required to take more classroom hours, and the exams mean everything."

"Plus, they can test you on anything," Brad added. "Show them you know something about literature, how the concepts of one generation, movement, led to the next and why the changes."

"I'm told feeding them back their ideas is the safest way to go."

"I've heard that, but I have trouble accepting it. Do they want to hatch a bunch of mimics who can't think for themselves?"

Art laughed. "You sound like me earlier this semester. I don't know what to do."

"Do what you think is right. That's all you can do."

Marilyn entered with Connell in her arms. "This girl's starving to death." She tested the formula and gave the nipple to the anxious baby whose wiry little body bobbed about in anticipation of dinner.

"God, she's beautiful." Art held one of her tiny feet. "Thank you both for one of the best Thanksgivings I've ever enjoyed."

"Hey, thanks for coming over," Brad responded, "and thanks for the help."

They walked to Art's car. "I saw you talking with Carl after that bitch called him a baby-killer. Was he all right?"

Brad shook his head. "He's okay. Carol and Bruce are caught up in all this anti-war stuff, but I never thought she'd personalize it like that."

"Clare's being here should help. Thanks again. It was great."

Driving around Norman, Art watched family celebrations, feeling distant, tied to nothing. Warmth and happiness, palpable, radiated from inside the homes, balancing his feelings of joy and alienation. He drove by

Judith's place on Faire Queene Lane, knowing she and her husband were in Muskogee. No one within, lights out, at least he knew a person who lived there, making him more than a total stranger.

On the kitchen table in the apartment, he found a note inviting him to join Carl and Clare at DeClines'. Too late; the drive had saddened him. He called and gave his regrets, using the exams as his excuse.

Both Saturday and Sunday he put in ten solid hours with the books. Late Sunday night Judith called. "We got back an hour ago. I wanted to hear your voice and find out how you're doing."

"I'm fine. Had a great time at Cunning's and put in some serious study time. It's good to hear you."

"Tuesday night, let's meet in my office."

"Sounds great."

Pollard, who'd answered the telephone, stuck his head out of his bedroom door. Clare had returned to Tulsa that afternoon. "Judith?"

"Yes," Art answered.

Carl came into the living room. "I take it you two have been seeing each other."

"You writing a book?"

"Matter of fact, I am," Carl answered.

"Kiss my ass and make it a love story."

"Just curious jerk-off. Do you have the stuff for your classes?"

"Right. Tomorrow and Tuesday they'll write themes. Here are the topics," Art stated, handing him the materials. "Tell them I want between four and five hundred words. Standard stuff. All the instructions are there."

"Good luck with everything. Remember, don't be a hero. There's no point."

The exams, administered in Kaufmann, started at ten and continued through two in the afternoon. Nora, Carl's friend, handed them out and explained the rules.

For the first exam, Art had ten topics from which to choose his three. Four were questions he'd seen on his mid-term exam in Manly's class. Two were directly from Manly's book on Hawthorne. He finished by 1:30, six blue books filled.

At the apartment, he ate, relaxed for an hour, then started on the books, concentrating on Yeats and Victorian writers. Carl graded papers. They said little.

On Tuesday's exam, he recognized questions from discussions in his

Yeats' seminar and from his mid-term in Victorian Literature. He finished a few minutes before two, confident he'd passed.

"How'd it go?" Carl asked when Art returned to the apartment.

"Easy, too easy. I recognized questions from the classes I'm taking and just winged through both days."

"Not the noblest way to go, but the smartest."

"I don't feel a twinge of conscience. I'm just elated to have it over."

"Here are the themes from your classes," he handed them to Art.

"Did you see Lauren?"

"Yes. She asked me to send her best and hoped all went well."

"If she sent her best, give it to me, and I'll take it to the bedroom."

"Are you celebrating tonight?"

"I have a little something planned."

"You might remember, I recommended getting your wick wet, not falling in love. In fact, you're the one who brought up the subject of jealous husbands."

"This is lust satisfying lust. Nothing else," Art assured him.

He'd been waiting for ten minutes at her office when she arrived, paper bag in hand. "Sorry I'm late. I had trouble getting away, then I went to Old John's liquor store to get a cold bottle of champagne."

"My favorite!"

After he uncorked the bottle and poured, Judith raised her glass. "To successful completion of your MA."

They finished their glasses and started with each other. He used her coat and his jacket together with other clothing to make a bed on her desk. She lay on it toward one end. He knelt on the floor in front of her and pulled her towards him, resting her legs on his shoulders. He kept his underwear on, afraid of splinters in strategic areas.

In the midst of feasting on her succulent moist flesh, he paused for a sip of wine. Bacchus and Eros combined to inspire him. He held her legs up and placed the mouth of the bottle in her vagina, slowing, carefully pouring wine into her. She gasped, squirmed, then squealed with pleasure as the wine's effervescence tickled her pink lips.

After filling her, he resumed his kneeling position and drank from her, lapping and licking to get all the wine he could. She became ecstatic with the physical sensations. "Oh! oh my god! this is wonderful! Oh, Oh!" She came before he finished the champagne. He grabbed the bottle and repeated the process. Before the third refill, he entered her. The tingling dampness created a sensation that shot shivers through his being and forced a gasp from his mouth. They continued until no wine remained.

In darkness, they sat naked, exhausted, holding each other. "That was the greatest present I've ever received," he said. "Let's patent the champagne glass."

She took his hand. "It is better to give than to receive, but I need to get going."

The champagne had made a mess on her desk and the floor. He used his shorts to wipe it up. "I'll toss my underwear and this empty bottle in the trash can in the men's room. That should drive the janitor nuts."

They dressed and kissed good night.

CHAPTER TEN

Gray December sped by, everyone preoccupied with the approaching holidays. For the last time, Oklahoma University carried its fall semester through the Christmas holidays, with finals to be administered during the early part of January. Next year, classes and exams would be completed before Christmas. Art felt ambivalent about the coming change. If he remained at OU, he anticipated the pleasure of a holiday season with no academic work hanging in the balance. But he'd miss the time to prepare for finals, write papers and grade Freshman themes.

Classes ended five days before Christmas for the break. Carl went to Tulsa for a few days with Clare, then on to New Mexico, Matt and Virginia took off for Colorado, Rick and Darlene for Boston, the De Clines for Arizona, Sugar's home, and the Cunnings to Omaha. Judith planned to remain in town until Christmas Eve day, when she and Larry would drive to Muskogee. She and Art met in her office each day before her scheduled departure, drinking wine and making love. He took care to deposit all empty wine bottles and soiled underwear in the various mens rooms in Kaufmann.

When they said their good-bye the day before Christmas Eve, he gave her a gold bracelet he'd purchased. She loved it and devised a plan to make it appear as though she'd received the bracelet from one of her relatives.

When she telephoned him later in the day, he found himself disturbed at her call. He'd prepared himself for their separation and was agitated when she asked to see him the next day. He recognized they were being imprudent, and the more time he spent with her, the more imprudent he wanted to be. Art expressed his concern, but she assured him she could get out for a short time without creating any suspicion.

That evening he thought about the intensity of their relationship. The boiling blood she aroused within him overcame propriety, discretion. He felt himself propelled by a force he'd never experienced, one so overpowering yet exhilarating, that he reeled to an intoxication produced by its marriage of dread and joy, a loss of self in the wet, stinging flesh of carnal obsession which suggested another plain of being, a oneness from two through annihilation of self. Whether or not this formed the reality he sought, in the midst of its power he soared beyond all his philosophical thrashing and self-doubt.

Yet, always, when released from this sweet oblivion, he questioned and doubted its completeness.

Christmas Eve day the weather turned around, and the balmy warmth became frigid. The temperature dropped forty degrees in three hours. Art had witnessed these dramatic weather shifts many times. Thus, while it held no surprise, it reminded him of another aspect of Oklahoma he hated. His VW, temperamental in the best of weather, wouldn't start. He bundled himself and walked to Kaufmann Hall.

"Damn, it's cold," he complained, taking off his jacket in her office.

Judith kept her coat on. He put his arms around her and tried to hug her body's warmth into him. He kissed her hair, which smelled of jasmine. She pushed her face into his chest and seemed intent on becoming part of his physical being.

"Into the yolk and white of the one shell," he commented.

"What?" she asked.

"It's a line from one of Yeats' poems. He refers to Plato and the idea that humans were originally spherically shaped and contained both female and male characteristics. Love is the attempt by the female and male to regain their original unity."

"That's beautiful."

"Perhaps it's true," he responded, still holding her as though she were part of him. "I never considered it a possibility until you."

"I have something for you," she said as she backed away from him and reached into her coat pocket, pulling out a piece of Kleenex.

"Just what I need. I feel a cold coming on."

She handed it to him. "Silly. Look inside."

She'd wrapped a small, tan colored pill in the tissue. "What's this?"

"Mescaline. Larry and I've done some. It's really nice, smooth, not rough at all."

"I'll be all right if I do this by myself?" Art asked.

"You'll have a wonderful five or six hours with no problems. Just be sure to do it when you have the time because you won't do anything else."

"Thank you," he said, holding his only Christmas present.

They kissed. "Can you stay?" he asked, going against his resolve.

"No, I told Larry I came over here to return some overdue books. I have to leave."

"Have a wonderful Christmas. I'll think about you, your hair, your eyes, your electric fur."

Art went to his dark, vacant office. The campus appeared deserted. He pulled a chair to the window and gazed at the bleak landscape. The low, gray Oklahoma sky looked ominous. The piercing wind blew stronger than the Chicago wind off of Lake Michigan. It controlled everything, even hope. Brown grass on the oval blended with red Oklahoma clay to create a rust colored carpet. "God, let it snow," he thought. "Cover this miserable scene." The soothing snow could soften the harshness, create a fantasy.

He took the bottle of wine he'd brought to share with Judith out of his jacket, pulled the cork and filled a dirty coffee cup. He toasted the cold, barren ugliness. "To your honesty, what you see is what you get," and drank. "Cold, heat; it doesn't matter." He knew the lie of the pathetic fallacy. It could not fool him. Art had seen too many men die in the face of the blazing golden sun, in the lush emerald grass. He remembered one such day, hot to the point of suffocation, the Saigon sun relentless, death's stench everywhere.

"I can't account for two of my men, Sir," Art stood before his OIC, Colonel Dunworth.

"The heavy fighting's been over for a couple days, Patowski. You'd better check the base morgue. They've got a lot of unidentified bodies there. Some lost their tags with their heads. Take a jeep. Tell 'em what you're doing. They'll let you in. If they're not there, go to the airport. They're using one of the hangars as a temporary morgue. We've got so many bodies they'll probably have to use another hangar."

Tet had raged over three weeks, but in Saigon there were signs of respite. Except for a few pockets of resistance, the fighting had lessened considerably around MACV Headquarters and the airport. Most of Saigon was safe. Chou Lon, the Chinese section, was the only place the enemy still controlled.

Art had been able to gather his men that morning. Four were missing. Later, he'd confirmed one dead and had found another in a temporary hospital outside of MACV. Though seriously wounded, he would make it back.

Art's hopes remained high. No one had seen the two missing men get hit, and their names appeared on no casualty lists.

Major Cherin, a thin black man about Art's height, ran the MACV morgue. "Before you go in the back, look through the name tags in my office," the Major suggested. "They were taken from the bodies of men who were brought here."

After a few minutes, Art found the name of Spec. 4 David Evans, one of his. Silently, he placed Evans' tags and morgue identification number to one side. He found no tags for his other man.

"If I might suggest Lieutenant, let's check Evans. They brought him in this morning. Then you'll have to look at the unidentified bodies. Unfortunately, there are many."

They walked to one of two storage rooms. The Major stopped before opening the door. "Understand this is an unusual situation. There's little room for the large number of men we've received. The Surgeon General is examining the effects of certain types of wounds, especially head wounds. The information they gather will aid in future treatments and in weapon design. You're going to see men who've been operated on. They won't go home looking like they do now. They'll be repaired or shipped closed casket." His eyes and voice conveyed compassion.

Inside, tables and stretchers were arranged around the room to afford maximum utilization of space. Each held an occupant in some state of disrepair. Some were covered entirely with sheets, others to the chest; some were on their backs, others on their stomachs.

Because of the dim ceiling lights, Art's eyes took a moment to adjust. He carefully moved behind the Major, trying not to look at each corpse they passed. Still, he saw many, some with their eyes opened, staring blindly at the ceiling, some with parts of their faces and heads missing. The even edges of many wounds indicated surgical procedures had been performed.

When the Major took an abrupt turn, Art found himself staring into a cavity that once held a man's brain, the entire top of the corpse's head and its insides gone. Art froze, the chill of death encompassed him; its smell filled him, bathing his face with its sickly sweet scent. He felt it coat his face, a thin film he'd never be able to wash off. He gasped for breath.

"Are you all right, Son?" The Major's question broke through Art's shock.

"Yes, I'm fine," came from his mouth, but the voice sounded distant and strange.

"Do you want to go outside for a minute?" the Major asked, touching Art's arm.

"No, I want to see if it's our Evans."

The Major walked ahead. When almost at the back of the room, he stopped by one of the tables. When Art reached him, the Major pulled back the sheet from the man's face.

"He's our man," Art said, barely audible.

The Major lifted the clipboard hanging at the end of the table.

"It wasn't pleasant for him," the Major started. "He got separated from his group, I suspect because of his wounds. Three fingers from his right hand were gone; he had a gaping hole in his right thigh. The VC tied him to a tree, cut off his genitalia and stuck it in his mouth. We're pretty certain he died before they got to him."

Art tried to rid his mind of what he'd heard, but his stomach muscles contracted and forced him to lean forward and support himself with both hands on Evans' table.

The Major placed his hand on Art's shoulder. "Of course his family doesn't need to know any of this. When you write the letter home, remind them what a fine young man he was, and tell them he died bravely in combat." He covered Evans' face and waited a moment for Art to regain his composure, "Let's see if we can find the other."

In a large adjoining room, body bags lined one wall and rose halfway to the ceiling, stacked like covered cords of wood.

"Those men have been identified and are going home," the Major commented. "The men on tables are unknown but have enough left of them that we think someone will be able to tell us who they are. Is this man black or white?"

"Black," Art replied.

The Major glanced at the first three charts without stopping. At the fourth table, he removed the sheet from the man's face. His nose and most of his mouth were gone. Enough remained for Art to be certain he wasn't his. After looking at two more bodies, Art peered ahead down the row of corpses. One, with its sheet up to his chest, appeared to be smiling. Art left the Major's side and walked towards it.

There lay Tyronne, his head resting on a thick pillow, looking as though he were enjoying a funny dream. Tears swelled within Art. He held Tyronne's cold hand under the sheet.

"I guess you found him," the Major said as he again touched Art's arm. "I know how close we get to these boys."

Art wiped his eyes. "He was a good kid. When did he come in?"

"Three days ago," the Major replied. "His head looks sunken into the pillow because the back of it is gone. A mortar or something big got him."

Art looked closely and saw the back of Tyronne's head had been severed, everything behind his ears gone. "It wasn't a huge beer can?"

"Pardon me?" the Major asked.

"Once we fought some VC with a couple cases of beer. I thought maybe..." Art couldn't finish, his words replaced by tears.

"Let's go back to my office. I need some information on him," the Major suggested. They turned and left.

Disassociated from time, Art had not noticed the failing light. He took the pill Judith had given him and washed it down with the remaining wine. In the street lights, he saw the falling snow. The cold had retreated, pushed on by the quieted wind, which whispered to him, "All is well, all is well."

Outside, Art enjoyed the mescaline's affect. He experienced euphoria and respite from the cold.

He walked in the snow to Campus Corner. All stores were closed; no cars were on the street; he was the only pedestrian. The neon lights from the Town Tavern, Orin's Pizza and other establishments created a panorama of brilliant colors. The greens, blues, reds and whites were joyful, radiating hope, possibilities, like the fresh wetness caressing his face. "My Christmas tree," he said aloud.

Art strolled around Campus Corner many times, marveling at the beauty of the snow, at the colors, at the wonder of existence, at the joy he felt, so happy to be alive.

CHAPTER ELEVEN

During Christmas break, Norman was transformed into a sleepy southwestern town. With students gone, the stores, movies, and fast food restaurants became friendlier, less impersonal places. Local merchants relaxed and exchanged smiles and cheerful greetings with their customers. For Art, the town almost returned to its 1959 facade of innocence.

Each day, Art allocated a specific number of hours for his tasks. After ten days, two term papers were ready for formal typing, the third lacked only a concluding statement, freshmen themes were graded, final exams for his freshmen were created, and he'd managed to prepare for his finals. This schedule meant no partying, not even on New Year's Eve, but he knew no one with whom he wished to party, and the discipline felt good.

The Saturday before classes resumed, Art received written notice that he'd passed the Masters' examinations and, upon completion of his current course work, would receive his MA. He celebrated with a bottle of wine and an Orin's pizza. The accomplishment vindicated his period of semi-Spartan-like existence. The small celebration, coupled with Sunday TV football, were appropriate rewards, simple gifts to himself.

When possible, he also used this time alone to search within himself and assess where he stood emotionally, intellectually and morally. He hoped this search would lead to a clear picture of his present state, an idea of where he wanted to go, and an understanding of the path he needed to follow. Through the process, he viewed past events with detached objectivity and focused on personal relationships, his association with the English Department and, always, the affect Vietnam had on everything.

He intuited that what he sought could not be obtained from people or institutions. Reliance on an organization, a professor, or a lover, appeared naive. The spiritual growth he sought must come from within, from his own work.

He recognized that the intensity of the passion shared by Judith and him allowed communication to a point, but, Art decided, the process suggested death of self with, at best, the creation of a new entity that contained the duality of man and woman. While romantic, Art did not believe this could result in wholeness, the self dissolving to a dew, awakening in a new form comprised of two, with this new creation equal to but greater than the sum of its parts, but with the parts lost as distinct entities. At a future stage in his development, this might make sense; now it did not.

He approached this process of introspection cautiously, as though exploring strange, new dimensions. Its revelations sometimes brought pain as well as wonder, appropriate for the birth of a new being.

Often, when reflecting upon the collage of his experiences in Southeast Asia, Art felt as though he watched a movie that included him. If not monitored closely, this detachment broke down and took him back to the fear and exhilaration of combat. When this occurred, he'd lose himself in time. Upon returning to the present, he'd discover himself bathed in sweat, heart pounding, shaking from fear and excitement.

One person understood the intensity of events Art recalled: Carl. But as with all experience, the actual realization remained private, locked within the individual's soul. Neither could fully comprehend the specific effect upon the other of even an identical experience. Thus, Art reinforced his growing belief that only he could bring order to the events that had occurred and to the events that would help define or discover him.

This solipsistic stance did not bring Art joy, especially since an instant replay of the last six months of his life resembled a Henry Miller novel. But although not pleased with himself, if there were anyone he could influence, it was himself, which lent his perception some element of hope, of possibility.

Sorting through the past semester, Art reasoned that his excesses were methods of responding to the absurdity and chaos with which he struggled. The throbbing intensity and exhilaration of sex provided the closest edge he could find to the fear and excitement of combat, deadly yet fascinating, filled with ambiguity.

Alcohol reinforced his belief in the need for an Aristotelian mean, the balance he'd sought his entire life. Alcohol provided a useful distancing effect, if carefully monitored. As with most things he enjoyed, he found it difficult to control, its excesses leading to escape from the consciousness he wanted but found so painful to achieve, its dual edge often more destructive than constructive.

On his way back to Norman, Carl telephoned from Tulsa and asked Art to join him the next week in a meeting with Pitts. He had asked Carl to chair a Freshman English textbook committee, and Carl wanted Art's help in forming the committee and making textbook selections.

Pitts greeted them with flushed face and his usual stagger. Motioning for them to sit, he fell into his chair, opened a desk drawer and pulled out a bottle of whiskey and three glasses. "Let's have an eye opener." He poured two fingers into each glass and invited them to partake.

"To a new year," he toasted. "I hope it's not as fucked up as the last."

Carl and Art laughed and drank the shots. Their eyes watered, but Pitts refilled their glasses.

"Were things that bad?" Carl asked, coughing.

"We lost five or six graduate assistants, " Pitts responded. "One was institutionalized, put in Central State Mental Hospital. Damnedest thing I've seen in all my years dealing with graduate students in English, who tend to be somewhat unstable anyway. It seems his amorous advances toward one of our first year GAs were rebuffed. They'd both attended a Baptist college in Shawnee for their undergraduate degrees. He was some years ahead of her, and they didn't know each other until she arrived here. They became friends, but this guy thought it was something more.

"She told him she considered him a friend, but that was all. He took it well. Everything seemed fine. Then, a week before Thanksgiving, she and a male friend were shopping together in Safeway and ran into this guy. He got hysterical, started screaming profanities; threw her into the frozen meats and tried to assault her with a Polish sausage. The other fellow tried to protect her, but the guy was crazed, knocked him out with a frozen ham. If it hadn't been for the store employees, Lord knows what would have happened." Pitts stopped and took a long drink of whiskey.

"Is the woman Linda Balker?" Carl asked.

Pitts squinted at him. "Yes, and remember, what I'm telling you is confidential."

"Definitely," Carl responded. " I knew she'd gone to Oklahoma Baptist University."

"At any rate," Pitts continued, "I've known this guy for five years, and other than the fact that he's interested in Eighteenth Century literature, he seemed fairly normal. I had him scheduled to teach three classes this spring, and I'm not certain Linda will return. So there are another six hours I might have to cover.

"We lost another one to pregnancy," Pitts stated. "She went home, Missouri I think, after little more than two months here."

Art, stunned, gulped down what remained of his drink.

"Would either of you like to pick up another course this semester?" Pitts asked.

"Yes, certainly," Carl responded. He and Pitts looked at Art, who remained dazed by Pitts' news.

"Hey guy," Carl shook Art's arm. "Are you okay?"

"Y.. Yes, I'm fine," he stammered, pulled back into the present.

"How about it?" Pitts asked.

"What?" Art answered.

"Are you interested in teaching another section of Freshman English?"

"That would be great. I can use the extra money."

"You have an MA?" Pitts asked.

"Passed the exams, and I'm wrapping up the course work with these finals," Art answered.

"Good! Then it's all set."

Pitts went on to discuss the Freshman English text-book committee and what he expected from them. He'd be their consultant, but putting the committee together and getting it to decide on which books to use were their responsibilities. While Carl took notes, Art sat numb, thinking of Melanie.

Before they left, Art asked Pitts about getting an individual office. Pitts assigned him to the one recently vacated.

"All his books and belongings are out of there, and he won't be teaching any time soon. Get the keys from Nora tomorrow and start moving in," Pitts recommended.

Pitts looked at his watch. "I have an appointment with a teaching applicant. Let me see if she's here."

He rose and opened his office door. The new teacher, a reincarnation of Hyppolita, entered. Over six feet tall, she had a dark complexion, its effect enhanced by jet black hair and eyes. In the cold Oklahoma January, she wore cutoffs, a black sweatshirt, no coat and sandals without socks. The baggy sweater could not hide her enormous chest. She glared at Carl and Art with palpable animosity.

"Wendy Gonaday, I'd like you to meet Carl Pollard and Art Patowski," Pitts offered.

They said hello. She grudgingly acknowledgment their presence.

"We were just leaving," Carl started. "Thank you for the help, Dr. Pitts."

Neither said anything to Wendy and remained silent until reaching the parking lot.

"Did you see that rack!" Art exclaimed. "I think she'll meet Pitts' requirements."

"She'd slit your throat just to see the blood," Carl countered.

"No kidding! I haven't seen a look like that since I told a friend she had to get penicillin shots for my cold. She has militant man-hater written all over her."

At the apartment, Carl asked Art what had happened in Pitts' office.

"I thought you'd gone catatonic."

"I think the pregnant girl he mentioned was Melanie, the girl I was seeing early in the semester."

"Is the kid yours?"

"I have no idea."

"Call her," Carl advised.

"Not that simple. She's a 60's woman. If she wanted me involved, she would've called. What's the story on this Linda?"

"She teaches a class next to me and told me about the incident. The guy went nuts. She'd tried to get rid of him in a nice way, but he was persistent as hell. Finally, she told him bluntly to get lost."

"I don't know either of them."

"She's a nice-looking redhead. I'm surprised you haven't scoped her out," Carl commented.

"One I missed. Just as well, though. Baptist ladies and I don't get along. I dated one when I was stationed at Tinker. After we made love, she cried and had to be saved by Jesus. Each time we did it, she cried and had to be saved. Does Linda cry and have to be saved?" Art asked laughing.

"I don't know, dickhead. Ask her. In fact, ask her to join the committee," Carl suggested.

"An excellent idea. If she comes back, I'll tell her you're our leader, and you recommended her. But there's not a chance anything can happen between us."

"Why?" Carl asked.

"First, she's Baptist, but more importantly, every time she looked at my cock she'd think of that Polish sausage."

Later, alone, he thought about Melanie. He decided not to call. If she'd wanted him involved, she knew how to contact him. If she were imposing order on her existence, his intrusion would offer only chaos. She did not need it, especially if he only sought to satisfy some vague sense of moral duty, moral duty that might not apply to the circumstances.

His new office was small, but private. He covered the inside of the glass pane in the office door with a poem by W.D. Snodgrass, "April Inventory," an expression of self and a way to keep prying eyes from the joyous activities he planned.

When he arrived with his last load of books, Judith greeted him. He quickly opened the door and locked it behind them.

"I missed you," he said as they embraced.

"Me too," she responded.

As they kissed, heat from his lust melted his ambiguity about their relationship.

"I can't believe you got your own office so quickly. I guess you passed the exams," she stated.

"I did. How was your vacation?"

"Fine, except I missed you terribly. How about you?" she asked.

"I accomplished a lot. It was lonely, but time well spent."

She took off her coat and hung it on the wooden coat rack. She wore jeans and a red sweater. He gazed approvingly at her fine ass. Over the past three weeks, he'd not allowed himself to dwell on sex, but here it stood before him, incarnate.

"You look great in red. It works so well with your eyes and hair." She smiled and sat in his lap.

"Too bad this place isn't big enough for a couch."

"I'm not certain I could make love with you in a conventional setting. The only time we're close to a prone position is when you're on a desk. Then I'm still standing. Doesn't anyone make furniture to accommodate this kind of situation?" he asked.

"I have no idea," she responded, smiling.

"Maybe we could start a cottage industry, furniture for fuckaholics," he continued.

Her kiss quieted him. Neither wanted conversation.

Under her jeans, she delighted him with a black garter belt and stockings. Trembling with excitement, he moved to a chair with no arms so she could sit atop him. Art's knees wobbled, almost deserting him.

She straddled him and with one hand held his penis and moved it across the opening of her pussy, raising and lowering herself slightly in simulated copulation.

"Put it in!" he groaned.

She smiled and let go of him, kneeling on the floor and placing his member in her mouth. Only peripherally concerned with his pleasure, she wanted to be certain of his full extension for her enjoyment.

He tolerated this sweet excursion for only a few seconds. "You truly understand the essence of enlightened self interest," he said with a shaking voice, as he lifted her to him and lowered her onto his anxious cock.

For two hours, Art lost himself in the magic of her body. Nothing existed for him but her beauty and the passion she engendered.

When both were sated, she remained seated atop him, their arms around one another, silent, taking comfort in each other's presence. Shadows from the trees outside the window left the wall and moved to the ceiling as the early winter darkness embraced all.

"Tell me about your vacation," he requested.

"It was all right. There's not much to do in Muskogee. I enjoyed seeing my family. How'd things go for you?"

"Quiet, got a lot done. Thought about us." "What were your thoughts?" she asked. "I couldn't take them too far. They always wound their way to the bedroom, or the swivel chair. Then I couldn't think about anything. Larry is giving me difficulty. He must know something is going on, and it can't do him any good. I thought about stopping."

"Our being together?" she asked, startled.

"Yes. It's starting to mean more than I'd planned."

She put her hand on his arm. "Is that so bad?"

"When sex was the only object, I felt nothing was being violated. With what I'm experiencing now, what I feel holding you after we make love, we're getting into another area, one that will lead to disruption and pain, things I didn't anticipate."

She remained silent.

"But I don't want to stop," he continued. "The sex is sensational, and being with you means..." his voice trailed off, "means much to me."

"I don't want to stop either," she responded.

"What about Larry? This has to hurt him terribly."

"He knows I'm seeing someone."

"Has he said anything?" Art asked.

"No, but he knows."

They remained silent, neither willing to make the break. After a short time, she left. He remained in the dark office for some time, resolving nothing.

On Wednesday, he both taught and attended classes. Lauren missed his class for the first time, but she had completed all of her assignments, so he didn't think much about it. He used the class period to answer his students' questions about the final exam he planned for them.

After teaching his last class of the semester, he retreated to his office to grade late papers and finish his remaining term paper. He answered the knock at his door expecting Judith. Lauren, eyes down, stood there.

"May I come in?" she asked.

"Sure," he answered, not attempting to hide his surprise. Dark circles under her eyes and a general nervousness did not alter her beauty or appeal.

"You look tired. Burning the candle at both ends?" he asked.

"Studying mainly," she answered. "I didn't get to your class yesterday and was afraid I'd missed something about the final."

"We discussed it, but you don't have to worry. I had a general discussion to ease fears, nothing specific. I'm asking for a straightforward theme, a little longer, but not much. I have to grade the damn things. How'd you find my office?"

"They have you listed in the directory on the first floor. Congratulations on the MA."

"Thanks. It's nice to have it out of the way. How've things been?" he asked.

"Fair."

"Are you still seeing Max?"

She started to cry. He remembered the last time she cried in a Kaufmann Hall office.

"What's wrong?" He placed his hand on her arm, but kept a platonic distance. "Can I help?" he asked as he handed her a tissue.

"Everything's gotten crazy," she said as she dabbed at her eyes with the tissue.

"Do you want to talk about it?"

She abruptly stood. "No, I have to go."

"You have a friend here. If I can help, let me know," he replied.

She smiled through watery eyes, a smile of appreciation, then grabbed and held him tightly for an instant. Before he could offer a response, she abruptly turned and left.

Momentarily, he considered going after her, then decided it would not be wise. Confused by the visit, he had too much to do to linger on its meaning. He did not leave his office until after midnight.

At his final, Lauren appeared tired but not as nervous as she'd been in his office.

He stood outside of the classroom and waited for the students to finish.

The last to leave, Lauren walked past him, not noticing him leaning against the wall. "Good-bye," he managed with a slight laugh.

She jumped, startled. "Oh! I didn't see you."

"No problem with the final?"

"No," she commented, a distant smile decorating her face.

"I'm sure you did well."

"Thanks," she responded.

"Not to be nosy, but are you seeing Max? You never answered me the other day."

"Five or six weeks ago, I moved in with him. It's been strange. He's working on a paper he hopes to publish, something about Descartes. Money's been a problem. The crowd he hangs out with is different."

"Are you happy?" Art asked.

"That's hard to answer."

"If you want to talk, remember my offer. I have no ulterior motives. Part of Max's problem is the time consumed by his work. Publish or perish is a reality, and it's not easy coming up with new ideas that are acceptable to the academic establishment." Art felt stupid defending Max, but he hoped to help her feel better.

"Has Max told you about Descartes' infamous brother, Maurice?" he asked.

"No," she answered.

"The Descartes family disowned him. He was quite a libertine, known for and proud of his flatulence. He changed his name to Desfart and used the motto 'I stink therefore I am.'"

She laughed. "Max may not appreciate that one, but Garnett will."

"You seeing a lot of him?" Art remembered Gary's interest in Lauren when they'd met at McGaw's.

"Too much. He's really crazy. Fun, but crazy."

They remained silent for a moment. Gazing at her, he remembered the reasons for the strong desire she once aroused. It awakened again, but as a distant memory, not a force upon which he had to act.

She looked at the floor, her awkward shyness reminding him of the girl he knew.

"You're incredibly beautiful. I hope everything works out well for you."

"You too Arthur. I know it will for you." Her eyes filled with tears. "I'd better run. I have another final in an hour."

Before she turned to go, he opened his arms wide. She stepped into them. He patted her back and held her upper body close. She clutched the back of his shirt tightly with her fists, then let go and quickly turned to leave. When at the staircase, she glanced back and smiled, her eyes loosening the tears.

A day after the semester ended, Carl invited Art to join him on a drive to Rainy Mountain, the hub of the Kiowa Indians' religion. Carl planned to write his dissertation on a Kiowa writer who'd won the Pulitzer and wanted to experience the place firsthand.

They left Norman late in the morning in Carl's car and headed for the Western part of Oklahoma. He told Art that the Kiowa believe their creation occurred when they crawled out of a log somewhere in the northern part of the U.S., probably Northern Minnesota or the area of Canada just above it. The tribe traveled south until they came to Rainy Mountain, which their priest recognized as the place for which they searched.

"It's sacred to them," he explained. "I'll try to talk to some of the people who live around there, but I've been forewarned not to expect too much. Their experience with the white man hasn't been exactly rewarding."

The mountain wasn't marked on any map. Carl knew its general area and a small town near it. After going through the town, he stopped at a few houses and tried to enlist the occupants' help, to no avail. Getting back into the car after his third attempt, he displayed some frustration, "Damn!"

"What's wrong Kemo Sabe. Indian brothers think you too pale to be trusted?" Art asked laughing.

Carl's exasperation focused on Art. "They have their reasons."

"You tell them, Kemo Sabe, that you chief No-poke-em-smoke-em?" Art countered.

"You're a riot, Asshole. Let's go to the mountain, if we can find it."

After wandering for a few miles, they recognized the dark mound jutting from the ground, its size dramatized by the surrounding flatness of the land. It rose to the clouds in harsh, majestic beauty, stark, unmarked, but unmistakable.

Rainy Mountain stood forty yards from the road. A deserted one-room Indian schoolhouse, in serious disrepair, stood to the mountain's east side. A barbed wire fence, five feet high, separated the mountain and school from the road. Carl pulled his car onto a wide grassy area off the road and up to the fence. "That has to be it."

They got out of the car and climbed the fence. Carl headed toward the mountain, Art to the abandoned school.

While Carl began to climb, Art walked carefully up the three steps to the schoolhouse entrance. He tried each step carefully and did the same with each footfall on the small porch.

The school's door gone, he stood in the doorway looking at the thirty by twenty foot room. The windows had no glass left, and the floor was filled with holes. For a moment, he felt transported back in time and imagined the many lives that had been influenced, perhaps shaped in this one room, what it must have meant to be brought in from the natural classroom the children, their fathers and their fathers before them had known, to be made foreigners in their own land and told to learn the strange new information as though it were the truth, the rules they now had to live by, as though the truths they'd known and knew did not matter, did not exist. He wondered if the sacred mountain helped blunt the injustice, the lie, the pain, the humiliation. He wondered if the sacred mountain's presence helped their truth continue within them, if its being were a reminder of their perseverance and the eternity of their perception.

Two steps into the schoolhouse a loud thrashing noise startled him. He stopped, frozen in his tracks. The noise stopped, but he could see nothing nor discern from where it had come, though at one point it had seemed all around him. He retreated to the outside. As he jumped off the porch, Carl, a third of the way up the mountain, turned to look for him. Art motioned for him to hurry down.

"What's going on?" Carl asked when he got to him.

"There's something in there." Art looked towards the schoolhouse.

Cautiously, they walked together up the stairs and into the school, Carl on the right side of the room, Art the left. Both peered into the holes in the floor, but neither saw nor heard anything. When they reached what had been the front of the room, they looked at each other and shrugged. Outside, they said nothing and began their ascent of the mountain.

They climbed in silence, watching for the rattlesnakes known to make Rainy Mountain their home. A soft, late afternoon wind pushed at their backs.

Halfway up, loud thrashing noises rose from the schoolhouse. As both men whirled around, a large white owl emerged through the school doorway and stood on the porch in regal splendor. Momentarily, it glanced at them, the intruders, then spread its wings and flew silently into the lingering sunset. Its wing span, seven feet across, gracefully and powerfully carried the bird toward the dying light. They watched in wonder as it blended then disappeared into the sky.

When they could no longer see the bird, they turned towards each other, struck with awe at what they'd witnessed. Silently, reverently, they continued to the top. At Rainy Mountain's summit, looking over the plains surrounding them, they experienced the place's holiness. For this time, they felt the oneness of all things, the unity the people of Rainy Mountain understood, the unity of time, place, matter, and spirit that few ever comprehend.

They traveled back to Norman in silence. Art could think only of the serenity and strength he'd experienced, marveling at the glimpse he'd been granted of another culture's beauty, wisdom and power.

Activity on campus increased as the mid-term break concluded. On the second floor of Kaufmann, Wendy Gonaday moved into the office directly across from the office Brad and Carl shared. She was the English Department's first militant feminist. She covered the top half of her office door with a reproduction of the Sistine Chapel ceiling, only God offered his outstretched hand to Eve, not Adam. At least that's the conclusion Art reached.

"It has to be Eve, who else?" he argued with Brad and Carl.

"I don't know, maybe Betty Fredian or Susan B. Anthony," Brad suggested.

Art looked closely at the picture, focusing on the lady's bare breasts. "Naw, Betty Fredian's tits aren't that big, and Susan B. Anthony never took her clothes off. Let's ask the source of this puzzlement." He bravely knocked on the door. No one answered. He knocked harder, but still no response.

"Carl, may I borrow your magic marker?" Art asked.

"What do you have in mind?" he asked, handing the marker to Art.

"Something's missing from this picture." Matt happened by the gathering.

"Hey. There all you dorks are. Let's get a brew."

"Good idea, Lava King. But first, look at this picture and tell me what's wrong," Art asked Matt.

"It should be Adam."

"Right," Art responded. "So let's take care of what's missing."
He proceeded to draw a large set of male genitalia in God's hand.
"Man," Matt asked, "who modeled for that, Harry Reams?"
"You certainly didn't," Pollard interjected.
"It looks erect," Brad commented.
"What good would it be otherwise?" Art questioned.
"You know she's going to raise hell," Carl commented.
"Well, you and Brad will be close by to calm her down."

CHAPTER TWELVE

Spring semester started with a bang, not a whimper: actually, two bangs, one caused by emotions, the other explosives.

Halfway through Art's Introduction to Literature class, angry shouting erupted from the second floor. Even with the door closed it distracted him and his students.

"I can't teach with that racket, and most of you can't concentrate. Let's call it a day, and we'll pick this up on Wednesday. Judging from the noise, I recommend all of you take the back staircase to get out of the building."

After the students left, he wound his way down to the second floor. A crowd had gathered around Carl's and Brad's office.

As Art made his way through the students, he noted most were laughing; a few stared curiously; one or two seemed angry. Pitts and Chairman Eldka stood between Art's friends and Wendy. Her eyes blazed with hatred and wrath. She pointed alternately at Carl and Brad.

"They defiled my picture, then they defiled me!"

Eldka stood facing her, speaking softly, trying to calm her. Each time Brad's and Wendy's eyes met, she'd attempt to dodge past Eldka and get to Brad. The Chairman, in his mid-fifties, proved surprisingly nimble and countered each of her moves, blocking her path.

Art noted a red welt rising over Brad's left eye.

"Dr. Eldka, Dr. Pitts," Carl started slowly, in a tone his close friends recognized as his voice of exasperation, "we did not defile her picture. She burst into our office and accused us, then physically attacked Cunning. It was totally unprovoked."

"You lying bastard! You have a magic marker in your office like the one used to mess up my picture!" she yelled.

"Every office in this building has the same kind of magic marker," Carl countered.

"Then they defiled my name!" she screamed.

"We talked about the derivation of the name Wendy," Brad offered. "We teased her a little, tried to get her to lighten up."

"First," she yelled, "they said my name had something to do with wind or windy. That took them to the subject of farts. The big ugly one said in Indian I'd be called lady who smelled foul. Then the beady-eyed one with the sweaty lip reduced my name to guttural sounds and started calling me Wa. First the picture, then me! I'll kill both the sons of bitches!" She lunged across Eldka at Cunning. The professor took the full force of her charge and reeled into the back of Pitts. All three would have fallen to the ground if Carl had not put his arms around them to halt their momentum.

"Don't touch me, you motherfucker!" Wendy howled. He released her left arm, which freed her to take a roundhouse swing at him. Out of instinct, Carl ducked. Eldka took the full brunt of her punch on the right side of his head. The force spun him around like a top. Wendy screamed. "Oh! Dr. Eldka! I didn't mean to hit you!"

Before he stopped spinning, Carl caught him around his waist and brought him to rest, holding on to assure he didn't fall.

Eldka's glasses hung from one ear. His eyes were slightly crossed, but he remained conscious.

Wendy, transmogrified, became a whimpering suppliant. Pitts and Brad concentrated their attention on Eldka's physical well-being.

Art stood among the crowd shaking his head and muttering.

"Tsk, tsk, what a shame such hooliganism should occur within this temple of cultural endeavor."

Carl saw him and glared. Eldka and Wendy went to his office, Carl and Brad to Pitts'. They agreed to meet after everyone calmed down. Before they were out of ear shot, Art addressed the crowd.

"One wonders what gets into those boys."

He went up to his office chuckling. Judith waited for him. "Hi kid, hoped I'd see you today."

He closed the door behind them. They greeted each other with a long kiss.

"What was that racket on the second floor?" she asked.

"One of the new teaching assistants had some women's lib problems with Carl and Brad. She got hysterical, even appears to have hit Brad. She took a swing at Carl and clobbered Eldka."

"Eldka!"

"Yeah, you have to admire her. First day on the job and she punches out her new boss. This is a monumental day for women's liberation. It should make the history books."

"It's a real zoo here. Did you see the janitor in front of the building?" she asked.

"No, I came in the back. You mean the Jesus Freak?"

"Yes, he's picketing with a poster that reads on one side, 'FORNICATORS REPENT', on the other, 'DRUNKARDS FIND THE LIGHT'."

Art beamed. "The fruits of our soiled underwear and empty wine bottles. Between the incident on the second floor and the janitor outside, I feel like an artist who has completed a masterpiece."

"What did you have to do with the incident on the second floor?"

Before he could answer, Carl knocked at the door.

"I hope I'm not interrupting," he stated in the same exasperated tone Art had heard earlier.

"No, my friend. We were just discussing your recent travails. Have you cleared up that sticky wicket?"

"Judith, I need to talk with him alone for a couple of minutes," Carl stated.

She looked at Art, concerned. "Hey, don't worry," he assured her, laughing. "Everything's fine. I'll see you later this afternoon."

She nodded and left. Carl closed the door behind her. "You could have spoken up down there."

"What do you mean?"

"When she accused me and Cunning of screwing up her picture, you could have said something."

"Like what? What the hell difference does it make if she knows who did it? Christ! You need to loosen up."

"I'm trying to get a Ph.D. from this shit hole. Incidents like this don't help the cause."

"Oh fuck! If you think this has hurt your Ph.D. hopes, I'll talk to Eldka. In fact, I'll go now."

"No, wait until things have settled down, but please talk to him. I'd appreciate it, and it's the right thing to do."

"I don't necessarily agree with your last point, but I will talk to him. By the way, Wendy threw a pretty good left. Got a lot of pectoral into it."

"She threatened to kill Cunning over the name thing, literally kill him," Carl stated.

"Has she settled down?" Art asked.

"She was so mortified about hitting Eldka, she became pretty humble.

Cunning apologized about the name, reiterating that neither he nor I messed up her picture. She seemed all right."

"You might say," Art added, "the wind was taken out of her sails." They both laughed. Carl turned to leave.

"Give it a little time, then talk with Eldka."

"I will, but it's hard for me to believe they're such petty people," Art commented.

"Eldka and Pitts aren't, but your pal Manly is a good example of the norm. They'll use any reason they can to get you. I've seen them do it."

"What's the story?" Art asked.

"It makes them more important in the overall scheme of existence, at least in their little realm of existence."

"Carl, are you sure you want to be a part of that realm?"

"I don't intend to be, but..." a loud explosion, close by, rattled the building. Glass shattered.

Art jumped to his feet.

"Damn, that sounded too familiar!"

"Jesus, it was close!" Carl exclaimed.

Both men raced to the nearest staircase. Before they reached the first floor, distant sirens cut through the winter air. Outside the building, across the oval, smoke rose from the Armory.

At the building, young men in ROTC uniforms supported wounded or shaken friends as they stumbled through the front doors, coughing, their eyes dazed. Art and Carl ran inside.

The sirens were close, but each knew the difference seconds can make. They crouched and made their way to the back of the building. Flames burned; two men remained motionless on the floor. Bending over them, they checked for pulses, then broken bones.

"Mine's still alive," Art called.

"Mine too," Carl yelled back.

Each picked up his man, Art over his shoulder, Carl in a cradle position, and hurried back to the entrance. As they reached the daylight, fire fighters came into the building and took the wounded men.

Carl and Art gagged from the smoke they'd inhaled. One of the fire fighters took them to oxygen units. After a few minutes, their breathing returned to normal.

"Good work, Fellas," the fire fighter offered. Art looked at him.

"I think I know you." For a second, they stared at one another.

"I'll be damned!" the fire fighter exclaimed. "You coached my youngest son in little league maybe five or six years ago. Jimmy Russell, a little tow head."

"I remember him," Art laughed. "He won a game for us in the last inning with a pinch hit."

"That's the kid," the father beamed.

"Is he still in town?"

"Went to Vietnam last week. He's stationed in Danang." Art's smile faded.

Hours later, back at Kaufmann, Art and Carl learned the toll: no dead, twenty-five wounded, six hospitalized, substantial damage to the Armory.

Classes for the rest of the day were canceled.

"That was too close to old times," Art commented to Carl.

"I know. What are you going to do?" Carl asked.

"I want to be alone for awhile."

"I'm going to Cunning's. Feel free to join us."

Art wanted no company. He walked to the nearest liquor store on campus corner and purchased as much Boone's Farm sparkling wine as six dollars allowed. At 89 cents a bottle, it was enough.

When Judith arrived at his office, he'd consumed four-and-a-half bottles. He could neither walk nor talk, the exact state he'd intended. She tried to distract him from the newsreels of his past that ran through his mind, but his incoherence made communication impossible. His pain flashed from one event, one person, to another event, another person.

Not even sex could distance Art from his ghosts. Frustrated, she left him there. Hours later, before finishing his last bottle, he passed out in his chair.

That night, he awakened in the jungle, the drop of sweat about to surrender him to the enemy. Trying to get the scream out, his fear intensified by the strangeness of the surroundings, the wind allowed the moon to appear from behind a cloud and gleam its virginal light through Art's office window, enabling recognition of his surroundings and escape from the jungle. Tears stopped, fear subsided, he smiled, alone but safe.

Before leaving to walk home, Art deposited the empty wine bottles in the trash bins in the mens rooms.

CHAPTER THIRTEEN

ART AND WENDY TAUGHT in classrooms next to each other. The first time they met in the hallway, she returned his smile. He considered it a major breakthrough, though he knew when she learned who enhanced the art work on her office door, her smile was doomed to become, at best, a scowl.

He waited a few days, then made an appointment with Eldka.

When Nora escorted Art into the chairman's office, two FBI Field Agents were with Eldka.

"These men are investigating the bombing and said they'd like to meet with you and Carl because of your actions at the Armory. Since our meeting was scheduled, I didn't think you'd mind taking a minute to talk with them," Eldka explained.

"Not at all," Art responded. Eldka looked relieved.

The older of the two men addressed Art.

"We know a little about your background, Carl's too, and thought one or both of you might have picked up on anything unusual the day of the explosion."

"We were in my office when it happened, ran to the Armory and helped get a couple guys out. I can speak for Carl when I say neither of us had time to scope the place."

"You didn't notice any suspicious looking characters, anyone unusual?"

Art laughed. "Suspicious looking characters! Have you walked around campus lately?"

Eldka smiled. The FBI men remained stoic.

"We tried to reach Mr. Pollard, but no one's answering the phone."

"Friday afternoon he drives to Tulsa. He's commander of the Marine Reserve Unit there." Art explained.

"Do you know where we can reach him?"

"He should be at the Reserve office tomorrow. He stays with friends when he's up there."

"Do you have their number?" The FBI man asked.

"No, I don't," Art lied.

"So right after the explosion you didn't notice anything unusual?"

"Sorry, nothing jumps out. Both of us took in some smoke. When we got out of the building, we were busy using oxygen the firefighters had," Art answered.

"If anything occurs to you, give me a call." The man stood and handed Art his card. They shook hands and both agents departed.

"Troubled times," Art commented.

"To say the least. In the years I've been here, nothing compares," Eldka commented.

"I'm afraid things will get worse. Speaking of which, I have a confession to make."

Eldka looked at him with a wry smile. "You planted the bomb?"

"Worse, I drew the male genitalia on Wendy's picture," Art confessed.

Eldka remained silent. Art looked at him and shrugged his shoulders.

"Your confession is commendable, but the secret will remain safe with me. I think she's settled down about it, and I can't see any good resulting from reopening the situation." Eldka's hand instinctively went to his jaw.

Art thought it best not to comment on Wendy's punching power. "I appreciate your decision, but I don't want Carl or Cunning blamed for something they didn't do."

"No one but Dr. Pitts and I know anything about it. I'll inform him, but we'll keep it to ourselves. If the subject arises with other faculty, I'll assure them that Carl and Brad are not to blame. In the future, take it easy with the graduate assistants," Eldka advised. "Generally, they're out there bouncing off the walls as it is. They don't need any help going crazy."

In the weeks that followed, when Art used the back staircase after teaching next to Wendy, he often encountered Jim the Freak from campus corner. They'd exchange greetings, but Jim, usually loaded on dope of some kind, said little more. Five years earlier, he had graduated from OU with a Math degree and took a job teaching at Norman High. Six months into his first semester teaching, the law busted him for selling weed to his students. Jim claimed he'd been framed by students who didn't like him. The jury believed the students and sentenced him to seven years. After serving over three, he returned to Norman and subsisted writing themes and term papers for students.

Daily, he and his German Shepherd sat in front of the Town Tavern, his radio blasting, his mind zoned from bad acid, talking to no one in particular, occasionally letting fly a batch of four letter words. No one complained, since he appeared to be harmless. For laughs, some people would say hello and pass a few minutes of incoherent conversation.

One day Jim surprised Art by stopping him as they passed on the staircase. "I'm in love," Jim groaned.

"Great," Art responded, "who's the lucky girl, 'Lucy in the Sky with Diamonds'?"

"No man, Wendy. Have you met her?"

"She teaches next to me."

Jim's eyes rolled back into his head. "Oh you lucky fuck! Do her vibes come through the wall and fill you with ecstasy?"

"Not recently."

"They will man; they will," Jim warned as he walked up the stairs moaning and talking to himself.

Art reasoned he should have known they were meant for each other. Both wore sandals and as little clothing as the law allowed irrespective of the weather. Both were isolated and zoned on society's injustices.

Years later, a sheriff in a small Oklahoma town would kill Jim. Unsympathetic to Jim's cries of pain, he heard only the four-letter words and stopped them forever, at least from Jim, with a bullet below his left ear.

But on this afternoon, Art perceived that all things flowed well in Jim's lopsided world. He'd found his soul mate.

Art learned Wendy had literally stumbled across Jim on campus corner. A conversation ensued and, quickly, romance.

They sped through a whirlwind, dope-ridden courtship. After a few weeks, she moved in with him, consumed vast quantities of bad acid and joined him on campus corner when she wasn't teaching. Her income allowed Jim to cut back on his paper writing and devote more time to drugs and hanging out. Nowhere existed a happier acid freak.

Art noted that Wendy's disposition improved after Jim came into her life. She still talked to few people, but the intense, hostile energy she once exuded disappeared. She'd found the man of her psychedelic dreams.

One late February afternoon as Art walked past her classroom, she came out with one of her students. He saw they were relaxed and enjoying their conversation. When she made eye contact with Art, he received a full, unqualified smile.

He walked absent-mindedly to his office, puzzled by her transformation. Judith waited for him.

"Do you have a minute?" she asked in her most official tone.

"Yes, just a minute before I have to get to the library," he responded.

Inside his office, they embraced. "What are you doing at the library?" she asked playfully.

"A study of literary eroticism in seventeenth century American poetry."

"That shouldn't take long," she replied, gently rubbing against him. They'd not seen each other for three days. The moment they touched, she rekindled the fire within him that extinguished all else, including, eventually, itself. The intensity blocked knowledge of everything but the excitement she created in his groin and of her, his proper heat and center, the creator and destroyer of this burning obsession.

For two hours they probed each nook and cranny of the other's body. Afterwards, sated, they sat holding each other's hands, not speaking, watching the shadows invade the office walls through the window.

"When you came up here you looked confused," she commented.

"I'd just seen Wendy. She and Jim the Freak are in love. She looked so happy. That's how I must look after we're together."

"That confuses you?"

"Yeah, the whole thing, Jim and Wendy, Art and Judith. Do we have to have another person to share life with to be happy? You've been told all your life happiness is only possible if you're sharing life with some guy. I have to find the princess I'll share bed and board with forever. Society makes us believe this stuff to perpetuate itself. It's depressing."

"Why do you say that?" she asked concerned.

"If we need someone else, does that mean we can't find fulfillment alone, by ourselves?"

"What else is there, if not other people?"

Her question disappointed him.

"If we must find another person to be complete, life presents awful contradictions. We begin with a separation that pulls us from primordial junk into the light of existence, alone. While others help us, hurt us, teach us in whatever they do, what is taken in and absorbed, what becomes part of the individual is his or hers, again, alone. When we die, we leave alone. Whatever level of consciousness is attained, it is there with the individual. No one else knows it, can see it, touch it.

"More and more I'm convinced that consciousness is the one attribute that explains our existence. We can talk about anything else, love, myth-making, art, symbols, technology, they're all related to consciousness. Without it, none of them exists."

"You don't think what happened in here between us is real?"

"Of course it is. The body, the mind, either or both are keys that can open doors to greater awareness, tools or paths, if you will. I think that's true. God, I hope it is! The intensity I experience with you blocks out other possibilities. It's so rich and full it destroys everything else."

She sat in his lap and snuggled close to him. They silently watched the night conquer the light.

At the apartment Carl prepared to leave the next day for Tulsa. "There's the evil gnome," he commented. "Thought you got lost."

"Judith and I had to do some cramming."

"Aren't you going a bit overboard on that?" Carl asked.

"Haven't we had this conversation before?"

"Just don't want to have to find another roomie because a dipshit got shot by a jealous husband."

A familiar voice shouting on television news diverted Art's attention.

"We will not allow the pornographers to invade our city. *Hair* will not be allowed to open unless we are assured there will be absolutely no nudity on the Civic Center stage." Skippy Sergeant stood on the steps of the Oklahoma City County Court House, the City's Attorney General behind him, nodding his approval and applauding.

"I don't believe it. That's the idiot I told you about from the Council," Art told Carl.

"What's going on?" Carl asked.

"It seems they're not going to allow the cast of *Hair* to take their clothes off," Art answered.

For the remainder of the weekend, each time Art turned on the TV he saw Skippy and the Oklahoma AG denouncing pornography, warning the producers of *Hair* that any public nudity would be dealt with harshly.

Late Sunday, with *Hair* scheduled to open the next Friday, the producers publicly announced that the Oklahoma City version of *Hair* would contain no on-stage nudity. Skippy and the AG declared a victory for morality over the forces of evil.

Late Monday morning, Art, alone in the Kauffman faculty lounge, finished a cup of coffee when Matt and Rouge entered laughing louder than usual. "Did you hear the news?" Matt asked Art.

"No, what?"

"This morning, Show taught his class in the nude. He was protesting the *Hair* thing."

"Oh shit! What happened?"

"The cops have been in Eldka's office for the last hour. We heard some of the kids left the class before it ended and called their parents. I don't know what happened to Show."

Later they learned Eldka had contacted Show before the law did and convinced him to check himself into Central State Mental Hospital for observation. This sage advice probably saved him from doing hard time.

The furor over Show's actions appeared in all the Oklahoma papers and made Skippy a celebrity. He lamented the Council's giving Show his prize for short fiction and reaffirmed that while Skippy ran the Council, a similar mistake would never occur.

Tuesday afternoon when the Freshman Textbook Committee met in the faculty lounge, everyone talked about Show's daring deed. The committee consisted of Carl, Art, Linda, Keith Drumright, Judith and Rouge, who Carl had ordered to join.

"I can't believe he did it," Linda commented to Keith, oblivious to his crazed, lovesickness for her. "Whatever possessed him?" she asked.

Gazing into and lost in the depth of her eyes, Keith did not hear the question. Art responded. "He wanted to illustrate graphically a dangling participle."

Linda laughed and threw her head back. "You're terrible! But how long will he have to stay in the hospital?"

No one knew.

"Did you hear the rumor that someone called the English Department and said there will be a repeat performance of Show's act, only this time it will be a female?" Linda asked.

"Any idea who it is?"

"No, but it will happen this Thursday."

Art concluded who the stripper would be, but kept his mouth shut, not wanting to be implicated in any way.

Carl called the meeting to order, and they quickly went through their assigned topics.

In an hour, they were finished and had received their assignments for the next meeting. As he left to meet Judith in his office, Art walked behind Linda and Keith.

"I don't mind walking your Russian Wolfhounds. In fact, I consider it an honor," Keith told Linda.

"You're too kind," she responded.

"I know what these winter winds can do to a delicate complexion. Do you want me there tomorrow at the usual time?" he asked.

"Around noonish would be wonderful."

"See you then."

"I must run," Linda said as she waved good-bye and left. Keith, in a trance, did not move, unaware of Art standing a few feet behind him.

"Are you alive?" Art asked.

Keith jumped. "I didn't know you were there."

"What's this about Russian Wolfhounds?"

"Linda has six of them. Her bitch had a litter. She breeds them. I've been taking them for walks, and now she's allowing me to walk them everyday."

"Allowing you? Don't you feel a might used?"

"Why? This way I see her daily and we talk. I think a relationship is developing. She's so beautiful."

Art knew this was a time to keep his mouth shut. "See ya," he said as he quickly headed for his office.

He'd been there a few minutes when Judith knocked.

"I've been waiting till the coast was clear."

They kissed, and he began to get serious.

"I can't stay, darling. Larry's going to meet me at the Student Union. I didn't want to leave without saying good-bye."

"The woman who plans to strip is Wendy."

"How do you know?"

"Intuition. I figure Jim the Freak put her up to it. She'll probably do it in the class next to mine."

"What are you going to do?"

"Shut my door and pretend it isn't happening."

"Wouldn't you like a peek?"

"Not enough to be involved in the mess that will follow."

Next Thursday afternoon, expecting trouble, Art kept the door to his classroom shut. Shortly after class started, noise and commotion erupted in the hallway. Jim had called both Oklahoma City newspapers and the *Norman Transcript* to alert them to the big event. Photographers were there to snap pictures before the Campus and Norman police arrived to escort naked Wendy to jail.

Wendy had told her class she planned to strip and teach nude in protest of the *Hair* decision against nudity and in support of Show. She said any or all the students could leave without penalty if her protest offended them. Of the twenty-five students, all but five males and one female left. When Wendy stood completely naked before the remaining six students, one of the males walked up to her and said, "Lady, you've got a lousy body," then departed.

She spent four days in jail. The City of Norman agreed not to prosecute provided the University assured the City that Wendy would never again be allowed to teach. No problem.

Two days after she taught nude, the English Department janitor appeared in front of Kaufmann Hall with a long table carefully placed to assure free access to the building. On the table were soiled undergarments, men's and ladies', and empty wine and beer bottles. Next to each item he'd listed the date he'd found the item in the building's trash bins. Two of his friends carried posters imploring all fornicators within the English Department to leave their evil ways and embrace Jesus Christ. The janitor handed out pamphlets and prayed aloud.

Wendy joined Jim full-time on campus corner. Her last public display occurred the following May on campus corner when she auctioned off her halter in an attempt to raise money to bring the Moody Blues to Norman. She got fifty dollars for her clothing, and one bare breasted picture of her found its way into an issue of *Playboy* magazine.

The Moody Blues never made it to Norman.

CHAPTER FOURTEEN

BRAD AND CARL APPROACHED their Ph.D. written examinations confidently. During the testing period, Art and Rouge agreed to teach their classes.

Matt's preparation for the qualifying exam, on-the-other-hand, did not go as well.

Between anxiety over the exam and recognition that his marriage seemed destined for the toilet, his behavior became increasingly bizarre. He supplemented his usual quota of beer and marijuana with a powdered substance he called Bosco, a chocolate flavored LSD that Garnett supplied.

Art provided Matt with occasional weekend solace, but stopped all weekday visits. He could not handle Matt's party pace, but neither could Matt; he started to miss many of his classes and other obligations.

When in Matt's apartment, they drank, smoked dope, commiserated on the English Department's injustice and woman's frailty. One Saturday evening, to make Matt happy, Art tried the powder and detected no affect. Still, Matt claimed it had magical powers, but his consumption of marijuana and beer made him an unreliable judge.

Discussing the upcoming exam depressed Matt, yet he talked about little else. The more depressed he felt, the more beer and drugs he consumed; the more beer and drugs he consumed, the more incoherent he became.

Virginia had left earlier, saying neither hello, good-bye nor her destination. Matt acknowledged her departure with a mumbled, "Good fuckin' riddance."

At 1:00 AM the telephone interrupted the cycle of consumption and mind foggy haziness. Barely able to walk, Matt stumbled to the phone and slurred "Yellow," into the receiver. After repeating his greeting three or four times with a few mingled profanities, he slammed it down in exasperation. "Ah shit!"

"Who's that?" Art managed to ask.

"Garnett, I think, but I'm not sure. He just screamed all the time."

"Screamed?"

"Yeah, he's zoned. Said the monster's moved in. Kept yelling the monster's moved in. Let's see if he's okay."

"We shouldn't drive."

"No sweat. He's in this apartment complex, moved in after his divorce."

At Garnett's apartment, lights were on and music blared, but no one answered Matt's polite entreaties.

"Fuck, I'll raise him," Matt slurred. He then banged and kicked on the door, while yelling Garnett's name.

After what seemed a long time, Gary answered the door. Tripping and loosely connected to reality, he recognized Matt, but not Art. With Matt's reassurances, they were allowed inside.

Newspapers covered the living room floor to protect it from open cans of black, red, yellow, green, blue and white paint. Five or six paint brushes lay scattered about. On the largest of the living room walls, in vivid colors, Garnett had painted a large mural of the Frankenstein monster seated on a toilet, holding a roll of toilet paper.

"Great art work! What's your landlord going to say?" Matt asked.

"You like it? It's why I called. I'd been in the bathroom for the last couple of days and forgot I'd painted it. When I came out, I freaked. After awhile, I remembered I'd painted it. Thanks for coming over, though."

Gary stood in front of the mural staring at the grunting Frankenstein, mesmerized by his masterpiece.

"Hey, Man," he addressed no one in particular, "would Frankenstein shit nuts and bolts?"

"Depends what he eats," Matt answered in stoned seriousness.

A 16mm projector, lights on but film long finished, continued to buzz, its white light illuminating the apartment's one bedroom.

Art turned off the machine. The room looked as though a tornado had swept through it. Beer cans, clothing, books and remnants of food were scattered everywhere.

The film's container had "Head Professor" XXX printed on it. "Sounds like a classic," he noted, taking the film off the machine.

He asked Garnett if he could borrow it. Gary didn't answer. Still standing in front of his creation, he could neither hear nor see him. Matt, lying on the couch, stared at the ceiling, mumbling incoherently. Art stuck the film in his jacket and left.

The next day he called Nora and asked her to meet him at the Department's audio-visual office. Because of his relationship with Carl, she agreed. He checked out a 16mm projector. In payment, he listened to her profess her love and longing for Pollard.

"He won't have anything to do with me because I'm married. His morals won't let him violate the marriage bed," she stated with conviction.

"Did Carl tell you that?" he asked, resisting an urge to ask if she'd looked in a mirror recently.

"He's said as much. You might remind him of the saying, 'If Mohammed won't come to the mountain, the mountain will come to Mohammed'," a saying she'd learned from her Iranian husband.

"Is the mountain an allusion to Carl's head size?"

She looked at him puzzled. "Just tell him."

At the apartment, Art set up the projector, got a six-pack and settled in, looking forward to an hour of raunchy sex. The first frame pronounced boldly that the film, a G&H Adult Production, starred such notables as Lottie Luscious, Happy Hooters, Harry Bawls, and Rod On. The first scene gave a professional panorama of OU's south oval, with coeds walking by, smiling for the camera. Some of the shots zeroed in on various parts of their anatomy, the ladies unaware of the camera's base interests. "Making porno flicks in good old Norman. That would knock the local gentry on its collective ass," he said aloud.

The next scene, inside a classroom, showed a professor in fake white wig and beard lecturing to his small class. He lamented the lack of interest in a subject as profound as sexual mores around the world. Since there were only eight students, he asked how they'd feel about meeting at his house, just off campus. The students smiled and nodded their approval.

Art stopped the projector and reversed the film until he found the face of a young blond woman. He froze the frame and studied it. After a minute, he recognized Lauren.

He fast forwarded the film and quickly found the group at the professor's house. They were joined by a women who pretended some claim to the professor.

Soon the house rocked with a full-scale orgy. Lauren, wearing nothing but knee high red boots and her blond wig, on hands and knees, delighted the professor with an enthusiastic blow job, while one of the male students took her dog fashion. The camera alternately zeroed in on Lauren's nob job, on her pussy being raked by the young stud, and on the passion-feigned faces of the professor and the young man.

Art again stopped the projector, this time concentrating on the professor. After a minute of study, he identified Max, Lauren's live-in philosophy professor.

The rest of the scene depicted the other three female students taking care of every sexual fantasy the male students could or would ever have.

The professor's lady, absent from the prior action, rejoined the group dressed in a black leather outfit that left her nipples and crotch exposed. She carried a whip and wore a chain wrapped around her waist.

Lauren, who had finished feasting on Max, received a sharp lash to her backside. A red welt indicated the whip was real. She started to crawl away, covering up with her hands to protect herself from the lady, but three of the naked young men grabbed her and carried her into one of the adjoining rooms and held her face down on a long wooden table. The woman proceeded to whip her, concentrating her efforts on Lauren's derriere. She screamed and writhed on the table as more welts rose on her backside.

One of the naked coeds joined Lauren on the table and began to caress and kiss her injured parts. The lash lady was distracted from her work by her husband who squatted between her legs, licking and kissing her private parts. Lauren and her comforter were soon involved in various lesbian sex games. The film ended with Lauren and her friend being joined on top of the table by four of the male students.

When Art clicked off the projector, he sat back confused. This attacked even his live-let-live philosophy of life. His budding arousal had changed to anger.

"What the hell happened?" he asked aloud. He telephoned a friend he trusted who owned a small photography shop. Art asked if he could do a favor and make a copy of an adult film, no questions asked. He told Art to bring the film by his studio on Monday morning, and he promised to have a copy for him in a few days.

After dropping off the film, Art called Max's apartment. Lauren answered. Although reluctant, she agreed to meet him for lunch at a Mexican restaurant they used to frequent.

He managed to find an isolated booth in the back of the place. She arrived late, nervous, agitated, unable to maintain eye contact.

"Lauren, what's wrong with you?"

"Nothing, why do you ask?" Her defensiveness was abrupt.

"You're so jumpy and preoccupied."

"If Max knew I were with you, he'd go nuts."

"Max is the reason I want to talk. I think he's taking advantage of you."

"How can you say that! He was there when you told me to leave. He took me in. He loves me."

"I never told you to leave, but that's beside the point. If he loves you, why are you having sex with every horny bastard in town? And on film, no less!"

She gasped. "What do you mean? You can't talk to me like that!" She rose to leave. He grabbed her arms.

"I'm sorry; I got upset, but we're not talking about your virginity. I saw the film."

Tears welled in her eyes as she sat back down. "Which one?"

"Damn! How many have you made?" he asked in shock.

"Two, we're working on another now."

"How'd this start?"

"I don't know," she sobbed, still not making eye contact. "Garnett has friends from LA who did films on the West Coast. We met them at one of Gary's parties, talked about money, did some drugs, one thing led to another. First they filmed me, then me and Max, then me, Max and Gary, then me and other people. It seemed innocent, just fun. Now I don't know."

"Do you want out?"

She hesitated. "Sometimes."

"Sometimes? How about now?" he asked.

"It's more complicated than you think."

"What's complicated? Are they forcing you?"

"No, they're not forcing me. I can't explain now. Let me call you later. But don't do anything, promise me."

"Why can't you talk now?" Art asked.

"I have a class. Promise you won't do anything."

"Okay, but I want to hear from you."

"I'll call you later today," she stated as she left hurriedly.

Art remained for a few minutes, lost in a strange kind of wonderment. He thought about her and then about his responsibility, his culpability.

She called in the early evening. "Arthur, how are you?" She sounded alert, relaxed and happy.

"Fine, you sound better," he commented.

"I thought over what you said, but I like the way my life is going. I receive five hundred dollars for each film, and I'm just doing on the screen what everyone does in real life."

"Lauren, you're getting paid to perform sex acts. There's a name for that, and it's not pretty."

"Don't be nasty. What do wives do? They get room and board for sharing their beds with men."

"With one man, he's called a husband. What's wrong with you?"

"You're just being unpleasant as..." Max grabbed the telephone away from her.

"Listen Crusader Rabbit, mind your own business! She's over eighteen, and no one's twisting her arm. You're just pissed because what you got for free is now expensive. She's wise to you, and she's happy."

"Max, I think the head of the Philosophy Department might ask you to retake a basic logic course or two. He also might have some problems with your extracurricular activities."

Max remained silent for a few seconds. "Would you do that to her?" he asked accusingly.

"Do what to her? You've got to be kidding! You're the one helping her make porno flicks!"

"Listen to you, Mr. Righteous. Who was the first guy fucking her? Who but Mr. Vietnam, killing innocent civilians, torching hamlets."

"Nice try, asshole, but Vietnam and Lauren are two entirely different matters. Let's ask your Chairman, an objective judge, what he thinks about the analogy."

Again, there was silence before Max spoke. "You were still first, right? Talk to her, see what she wants."

After a minute, Lauren came back on the telephone. "Can I see you tonight?"

"Sure, but why?"

"I want to explain some things. I'll be by your place in the next hour or so."

She arrived in twenty minutes, looking great. She wore the knit dress she had on the first time they had sex.

"Nice touch," he thought.

"It's been a long time since we've been together here. Where's Carl?"

"In the middle of his Ph.D. exams; he's studying late every night."

"Good, I hoped we'd be alone."

"Would you like a glass of wine?" He poured two glasses and handed her one.

"Thank you," she sipped from the glass. "Now let me offer you something." She took a baggie out of her purse. It contained white powder he'd not seen before.

"What's that?" he asked.

"Cocaine." She poured some onto a mirror, then used a razor blade to separate it into five lines. "I'll show you how to do this." She used a rolled bill to snort two of the lines, then handed the bill to Art. He emulated her actions, noting it was a one hundred dollar bill.

"Go ahead, do the other one," she encouraged.

"Are you sure?"

"I have plenty," she held up the baggie, still half full.

They did five more. Art experienced his first cocaine high and liked it.

"I do this all the time. It's great."

"How expensive is it?" he asked.

"Very! At least compared to pot or acid."

"If you quit making porno movies, you can get stoned like most of the people around here."

"I like what I'm doing, and I don't want you messing it up. Please."

She rose and brought the cocaine and accessories to him. They each did two more lines. When he tried to hand her the one hundred dollar bill for the last line, she slid into his arms, kissing him and hungrily putting her tongue deep into his mouth. At the same time, she stuffed the hundred dollar bill into his shirt pocket.

"I want to blow you," she whispered.

It felt too good. He starred in the movie. "Art Pole On," he said out loud, laughing but pushing her away. "I'm not going to be part of this any more than I am."

"Arthur, what's wrong? You won't do anything, will you? I'm happy, making lots of money, not hurting anyone."

"What about yourself?"

"I'm fine, really happy."

"I won't do anything, not if it's what you want."

"Promise me," she pleaded.

"Promise," he handed her the hundred dollar bill.

"I know you need this," she said.

He shook his head and stuck the bill in the top of her dress. "Between teaching three classes and fucking only married women, I've been able to keep expenses down. I'm actually saving money." She didn't laugh. "Lauren," he continued, "one of the reasons I want to teach is money doesn't mean a lot to me, at least it's not a primary objective. I'd like to think I can't be bought, and that's what you're trying to do. I won't make trouble, but I won't condone what you're doing."

She ignored his last remark. "Do you want the rest of this coke?" she asked.

"No, I liked it too much. You'd better watch that stuff."

"It can't be that bad; even Cole Porter sang about it. Promise you won't cause trouble."

"Is Max worried?"

"Please?" she responded.

"For you, I promise, but be careful. The whole thing's a recipe for disaster."

The next day he picked up his film, stuck it in the back of his closet, and asked McGaw to return Garnett's copy. He said nothing about the episode to anyone, but he had difficulty getting the situation out of his mind, debating whether his silence constituted a sin of omission, not against a societal standard, but against Lauren.

He and Judith continued to make love and drink wine in his office two or three times a week. For the janitor's benefit, Art continued to place the empty wine bottles and soiled underwear in various trash bins around the Department, sometimes not disposing of them until during the day to keep the holy roller off track.

Art found this semester much easier than the first. He enrolled in only two courses, and the classes he taught were all introduction to literature courses. Most of the reading material he knew well. Between revelries, Judith and he discussed literature and teaching. Both learned that most of the students favored short stories. They thought them more straightforward and easier to understand than poetry or drama. Despite his love for poetry and interest in drama, to accommodate the students, he concentrated on fiction.

He discovered a jewel in the freshman anthology, Salinger's "For Esme with Love and Squalor." It touched Art because of his association with both of the story's major protagonists. The story is set in Europe at the close of W.W.II. One of the central characters is a soldier who, near the end of the story, is close to a nervous breakdown.

A young girl, Esme, whom he met in London before he shipped into battle, is his salvation. Through all of war's devastation, the death of her pilot-father, the added responsibility she must assume in taking care of her little brother, the nightly bombings, she hangs on by her ragged, bitten fingernails, the only ostensible sign of her anxiety and stress.

For Art, she represented the personification of Hemingway's concept of grace under pressure. At the story's close, in war-torn Europe, as the soldier is close to a mental breakdown, he receives a package from her that contains a letter to him and her father's watch, her only material remembrance of him, as a gift. The child's ability to give of herself irrespective of her circumstances, rocks the man back into perspective. Through her strength, he remembers himself and survives.

In teaching the story, Art explained how voice and action work together to establish perspective. How subtle nuances of language develop the characters and exhibit their strengths and weaknesses.

He took four class sessions to work through the brief story, but the students seemed to enjoy the process.

In his last lecture on the story, Art devoted fifteen minutes to his conclusions about the story. Per his usual practice, he did this with no formal lecture notes. He had general ideas written down and expanded upon them. The class, enthralled, hung on every word. When finished, two or three minutes remained. "Are there any questions or comments?" he asked.

When no one spoke, he started to dismiss them, but a young woman raised her hand.

"Have you ever acted on the stage?" she asked.

The class waited for his response.

"There's one leaving in ten minutes, and I'm going to be on it," he said, as he grabbed his books and departed.

In his office, he thought about the student's question and how it reminded him of his isolation, the frame of reference that would always separate him from others. "No matter," he decided, "an avenue of communication had been constructed." He'd helped them see Esme's strength and the salvation it effected. In a small way, they'd experienced a part of his anguish and hope.

The night after Brad and Carl took their last test, both were mentally exhausted. Because of the schedule, Carl did not go to Tulsa. Clare came in on the bus, arriving in the early evening.

All of their friends met at Cunning's place to extend some support. At a somber gathering, Carl and Brad expressed their relief the tests were over, and confidence in their performances, but admitted anxiety, knowing the arbitrary nature of the grading process. Rouge, angry at Art and Matt for passing out No-dose to his students before he taught his morning class, spoke only when addressed directly. His wife made certain she stayed in a room other than the one occupied by Art or Matt.

Art missed Judith. Matt got drunk as quickly as possible, occasionally blurting out misgivings about the qualifying examination he had to take in a few weeks. Virginia was not with him. Rob and Sugar arrived shortly after a tiff over some minor issue. Only Mary, Clare and the children were in decent moods. The women gathered in the kitchen, while the men lingered in the living room watching television.

Carl sat in a large lounge chair, a beer in one hand, vacantly staring out at nothing. Art walked over and stood in front of him. He stooped to glare directly into Carl's eyes. "You look dumber than usual. What's wrong, brain rot?"

"Today we were tested on American lit. I don't trust Davies. He's a snake and doesn't like me."

"Davies doesn't like anyone but Davies. Give it a rest. You brown-nosed him enough to get through," Art responded.

"What were you doing with that 16mm projector?" Carl asked.

"Nora tells you everything. Actually, I got a dirty movie, a couple of six packs, and had a whack-off party."

"Whack-off party?" Carl asked.

"Yeah, you know, the old circle jerk. When you were a kid, remember?"

"You masturbated?" Carl looked at him in disbelief.

"Everybody did when they were kids," Rob interjected.

The other men nodded in agreement.

"I never did," Carl stated.

"Never?" Rob countered, amused at Carl's disclaimer.

"No, never!"

Art laughed. "He had the enlisted men do it for him. That's why he keeps Red Dick around." Rouge failed to see the humor. "Remember your eighteenth century literature; to whack is human, to get laid divine."

Carl looked at Art quizzically, then said disgustedly, "Get out of here you miserable wretch, or I'll tear your fucking throat out."

Art turned his back to him and farted. He started to run, anticipating instant revenge. He'd gone five or six steps, but heard no pursuit. Carl, unmoved, simply fanned the air with his hand. Art looked at Rob. "This is serious."

They walked to the rear of the house where Scott, Cunning's youngest boy, played by himself. Art told Rob to gather all the adults around Carl. In a few minutes, Scott walked up to Carl, tugging at his shirt to make him aware of his presence. He smiled at the boy. "Hello Scott, what can I do for you?" he asked wearily.

"Don't worry Mr. Pulyard. Give professor Davies bowjob and evewyting be aw wight," the child responded, patting Carl's leg and smiling in his innocence.

The men, with the exception of Brad, roared. The women retreated to the kitchen. Brad picked Scott up and cradled him.

"Thank you for trying to make Mr. Pollard feel better," Brad said. Scott smiled broadly, enjoying the attention.

The rest of the evening, if not riotous, was relaxed. Clare planned to stay over at Carl's, with Art bunking elsewhere. He assured Carl he had plans, intimating a lady's involvement, but, through sheer procrastination, had neglected to arrange anything. He left before any of the others and picked up his shaving gear and a change of underwear. He went to his office and worked on his play, rewriting late into the evening. He slept in his office chair, awakening early with the first rays of sun.

Saturday, he remained on campus, grading papers, writing and going to the library to relax, reading whatever caught his fancy. In early evening, he walked to campus corner and purchased jug wine and chips. Half-way through the bottle, the world looked less ominous, but no less lonely. He called Judith's house. Luckily, she answered.

"You wanna go out tonight?" Art asked.

"Where are you?"

"The library, a little drunk."

"Larry's there too, working on a paper."

"Maybe we can double date," he quipped.

"Pick me up. We have two or three hours."

As darkness enveloped Norman, he found her waiting outside the house. In a few minutes, he'd checked them into a motel.

They shared the rest of his wine and made love. After two hours, both fell asleep. He awakened, still drunk. The star spangled banner played on the television. He grabbed his watch. It read 1:30 AM. She stirred with his movement.

"What time is it?" she asked.

"We screwed up." He rose and pulled on his pants.

In the car, they said little. He wondered if Larry would be outside waiting and what would ensue.

"Do you want me to go in with you, if he's not outside?"

"No, let me deal with this," she responded.

"It doesn't seem fair to you. I don't mind. I don't like it, but I don't mind."

"Drop me off in front of the house and go on," she insisted.

He looked at her, searching for a sign of uncertainty. He detected none.

Her house was the only one with lights on. She got out of the car and never looked back. He waited till she was in the door, then left.

Back at the motel, he thought about everything they'd done. Their actions and inactions spoke for themselves.

Art sweated through Sunday anticipating Judith would tell him Monday morning what had happened. She called in sick, extending and increasing his anxiety. He imagined Larry beating her, then coming after him with a gun. With or without his imagination, a confrontation seemed inevitable. He both dreaded and welcomed it. Adrenaline flowed through his body.

His fantasies alternated between fights with Larry and life with her. He won the fights. She then rewarded him with wild, abundant sex, laughter, and reinforcement of his creative interests. Together, they flourished, had it all.

In the midst of these daydreams, a student walked past his open office door carrying a small radio. On it the Beatles sang "When I'm 64." Art listened until the music faded.

At 28, 64 seemed ancient, a distant planet to which he might or might not journey. But, he thought, if I live that long, who will I be? The skin, the hair, the body will be different, the inexorable ravages of age. My eyes will be the same, but they'll see events, people differently from the way they see them now, saw them yesterday. Experiences will be assimilated, learned from and used as guides. This voice from my mind will be the same consciousness that's guided me this far, but it should be richer, more in tune with itself, its surroundings, better able to discern and make decisions. Choices will be more clearly defined, perhaps easier to make.

He scoffed at this last thought. Choice is rarely easy. It always involves giving up something, letting go of some option. Deciding what to abandon is the hard part of the road not taken.

He remembered decisions he'd made, things he'd done that he'd do differently if given the opportunity. The things he'd do differently were the things that defined him, explained his identity at that moment in time. This realization, true now, would be true thirty-six years from this day.

How satisfying it must be to make the right decision, one that a person can live with for sixty-four or three hundred and sixty-four years.

Thus far, his decision-making process left much to be desired. He recognized that intelligence and knowledge are useful tools in the process, but, for him, the perception that comes from experience seemed to be key. "It's called learning things the hard way," he said aloud.

A knock at his door interrupted the reverie. A man two or three years younger than he, about his size with light brown hair and a troubled countenance, stood in the doorway. Art rose and approached him, never losing eye contact.

"Larry?" he asked as he extended his hand. "Come in and sit down." The young man unenthusiastically shook his hand and sat.

Art closed the office door. "I'm sorry about Saturday night. It was totally out of line."

Larry looked at the floor. "Out of line! I guess! You're just fucking her. That's all it means to you. You don't care about the fact we're married, nothing!" His voice rose as he talked. Art remained calm, sensing he could control the situation if he kept his head.

"It started that way. It grew to mean something more. I didn't see it coming."

"Just leave her alone! Don't see her again!" Larry's voice grew louder. Art thought tears were close, and he experienced Larry's pain.

"I know this is asking a lot, but I do care about her. I'd like to talk through some things with you."

Larry's appearance changed. Art saw his underlying fear, not of him, but of losing Judith. "Like what? You should simply agree to stay out of her life. End of story!"

"It's not that simple. Wouldn't it help all of us to understand how the hell this happened?"

He didn't respond.

"Do you mind if I ask how long you've been married?"

"What's that have to do with anything?"

"I thought that after some period of time, boredom can set in." He did not intend to add to Larry's humiliation with statements about his physical problem. "I'm just trying to understand what happened. I've never been involved with a married woman before."

Larry glanced at him, then looked down. "We met right after the breakup of her second marriage. She moved into the apartment upstairs from me. I saw a line of guys you wouldn't believe. A different one every night. She and I kept running into one another, started talking, one thing led to another, and we were dating. With me it was spiritual, what she thought she needed. What a joke."

"I don't think it's a joke."

"What did you make it?" Larry shot back. "I'm not too literary, but I think the expression 'I wear horns' applies." He walked to the window and looked out. "I love her, though, and I want you out of my life."

"That's what you want. What does she say?" This was as close to a direct challenge as he intended to get.

Larry didn't turn to address him. "She says she loves me, but right now wants to be with you, Mr. Wonderful, Vietnam vet, writer, English Department whiz. I'd like to see you after a year with her. Guys always coming on to her, the demands she makes. I wasn't nearly as experienced as she, but things were going okay, we were happy. Then at a party about a year ago, she got high and fell into bed with some ex-jock she knew. I caught them in the act. He yelled at me to get out. I stood there with my mouth hanging open, looking more stupid than usual.

"She promised it wouldn't happen again. But things went downhill from there, at least they weren't the same."

"Are you sure you want to stay together?"

Larry wheeled around, fists clenched. "Yes Goddamn it! If you'll leave us alone, we'll be fine!"

Art knew this wasn't true, but he could not write the scenario. He remained seated, trying to focus on what would drive his decision. What salient factors should he consider, the ache she created in his loins, the pain he saw before him, the relationship of two people, Judith and Larry, Judith and Art? He thought about their silence Saturday after awakening in the motel, neither willing to commit; he thought about what Larry had just told him.

"All right," he began slowly, carefully. "I will stay away from her, but I want you to know there is pain in this for me. Walking away from her is not easy. "

Larry's face expressed his amazement at Art's acquiescence. "I'm, I'm glad you understand, that you're willing to do the right thing."

Art stood. Their faces were inches apart. "I hope it's the right thing. At any rate, you have my word. We won't see each other again, at least not intimately." He opened the door.

As Larry passed him, he glanced as though he had to check to see if Art were being honest. "You'd better mean that," he blurted out with what authority he could muster.

Art, not threatened, looked directly into his eyes. "You have my word."

An hour remained before the freshman textbook committee meeting. He opened his office window and let the brisk late March wind enter. The trees outside remained bare. He noted few buds on any of the foliage had ventured forth. Nature did not believe the March promise of spring. But looking closely at the branches of red buds and dogwoods around campus, Art saw hints of colorful explosions to come. His White Sox had been in spring training for over a month, and in ponds, trees and bellies, new life strained to awaken, so much pregnant with the tenor of birth and rebirth.

He arrived at the faculty lounge ten minutes late. Only Linda, Carl and Rouge were there.

"Where are the rest of us?" he asked, not surprised at Judith's absence.

Linda looked away from him. Carl growled, "Let's re-schedule the meeting for next week. I'll call Keith, Linda call Judith."

The gloom in the room was palpable. He sensed theirs, but his own concerns kept him from asking anything.

"Linda and I were just going to the Student Union for a cup of coffee. Want to join us?" Carl asked Art and Rouge.

"Thanks but no," Art responded. "I've tons of papers to grade and poignant prose to pursue," he said as he held the back of one hand to his head. Rouge also declined.

Later that night at the apartment, Carl explained why Keith Drumright missed the meeting.

"Before he went to walk her dogs, Linda called and told him she had something special for him, something he'd wanted for a long time. It would be her way of showing her appreciation for all the help he'd been. I know Keith thought he'd finally nail her. He probably pole vaulted all the way over to her house. When he got there, she presented him with one of the pups. That's what she was giving him."

"Did she say how he reacted?" Art asked.

"She said he was quiet and didn't seem grateful. He took the puppy without saying a word, not a thank you, adios, nothing. When he opened her front gate, the dog jumped out of his arms, ran into the street and was hit by a car, died instantly."

"The guy was in shock. He thought he was going to get a pussy and he got a puppy. Did she understand what upset him?" Art asked.

"Not a clue. I tried to explain."

"How'd that go?"

"All right, but who knows. What's with you and Judith?"

"It's over." Art explained what happened Saturday night and went through the meeting with Larry.

"Why don't you come to Tulsa one of these weekends. Clare works with a bunch of beauties. Surely one of them would be interested in a wily gnome," Carl added.

"Right now I want a respite. It's been a very bad year with women."

The next day Judith waited for him at his office. After he closed the door, they kissed, but this did not lead to their usual activity.

"Sit down," he said. How's it going?"

"Fair. Larry's settling down. He told me about his meeting with you. He said you agreed not to see me."

"That's right. It's over between us."

"Why? Don't say that! You're not afraid of him."

"No, I'm not. I am afraid of something, but not him," Art stated.

"Of what?" she asked.

"You. Before yesterday, I thought a confrontation would clear everything. One way or another, when he left my office you'd be mine. But he told me what happened, about walking in on you and the ex-jock. It didn't take Freud to figure out why he's having impotence problems. You did it to him, you cut his balls off. I helped you do it again. I'm not into that bullshit. What's more, you lied to me. You told me you didn't know what happened to him." He stopped; she remained silent.

"Another thing," he continued, "our silence Saturday night. If we cared, we would've stayed together and gone to see him Sunday. We weren't willing to do that. Neither of us will commit."

"I will, right now," she said with urgency, leaning forward to put her hand on his arm.

"I will not," he stated firmly, with no trace of equivocation.

"Please," she pleaded.

"No!"

She walked to the door. Without facing him, she said, "I love you," and waited. When he didn't respond, she left.

CHAPTER FIFTEEN

ART HELPED CONTROL HIS OBSESSION for Judith by watching the dynamic campus scene. Not surprisingly, he observed that the Armory bombing did not affect campus life as the radicals thought it would: Most students willing to chant anti-war slogans and carry peace signs were not willing to kill people. It's one thing to be in style, but another to take that style to its logical conclusion. Art listened and watched as the daily chanting and picketing continued, but noted that the number of students participating had diminished significantly.

His position on the war remained an enigma to his students. The Armory episode had made him and Carl local heroes. Complimentary articles about them appeared in the *Norman Transcript* and Oklahoma City newspapers. They were cited as Vietnam veterans who again had put their lives at risk for comrades in uniform. But when asked his views on the war, Art voiced misgivings and, if pressed, launched into his historical understanding of the mistakes that had led America into Southeast Asia.

In the next breath, he'd praise the Americans in Vietnam, citing their heroism and the unselfish sacrifices he had witnessed. Questioners left confused.

Many of Art's students believed that to receive good grades they had to be politically correct, whatever that meant. They thought this more important than knowing how to write a well structured, grammatically correct, six-hundred-word theme.

This perception was wrong. Art graded their papers on the basis of structure, logic, and grammatical correctness. Yet, students who failed never found fault in their abilities, only in Art's imagined politics.

One such student made the mistake of telling Art he had to pass or he'd lose his student deferment, the 2S warranty keeping him out of the jungle.

"You'll be graded like everyone else," Art told him. "If you don't pass and lose your deferment, the failure is yours, no one else's."

Art tried to disguise his anger at the student's attempt to make his personal safety Art's responsibility, at the young man's inability or unwillingness to take control of his life. The student mistook Art's civility and tried to argue with him. Big mistake! Art lost control and stood shouting, "I recommend you add to the list of your murderers your high school English teachers, all your grade school teachers, and include your mother and father for conceiving you!" The student left abruptly and never returned to Art's class.

Part of Art's heated response resulted from the inequity he thought the 2S Deferment represented. He viewed it as the epitome of social injustice, America's way of telling college students they were better than men their age who didn't go to college. He thought this logic presumptuous and antithetical to America's professed core values.

Conversely, he knew Vietnam had turned everything upside down. The men and women who cared most about the abstractions the USA represented were the ones sacrificed, the ones cynically wasted for politicians' and politician-warriors' blurred goals.

Art knew that most who survived the experience would never again trust anyone in authority, civilian or military, a position they might have reached with age and wisdom. He also knew that ultimately, each had to arrive at his own conclusions, make his decisions and live with and learn from them. This understanding kept Art from maudlin concern over his comrades' fates and from despair over his own.

The duality inherent in these issues created a constant struggle within him. Yet out of these unyielding dialectics, he recognized the individual benefit that could be realized. It involved knowledge and understanding of self, recognition that reliance on anyone or thing to determine the essence of one's existence would not work. What finally mattered, what had to be trusted, came from the individual human heart, from the experience of being human, taking chances, making mistakes, but, through the experiences, accepting responsibility, remaining open to possibilities, and groping to find the essential elements of existence. Then, even after losing to the point of devastation, after mistakenly believing lies that could lead to involvement in a misadventure like Vietnam, the individual could understand his culpability, learn from his mistakes, forgive himself, forgive others, and find the will to not merely survive, but to persevere, and, perhaps, to understand.

Yet no matter what level of spiritual enlightenment he sought, Art acknowledged the strength of physical passion as a force that contended within him to reign over his existence, no matter how obvious the conclusion. He found the crisis in his crotch unyielding. His passion for Judith boiled in his gut. Staying away from her proved difficult. When they passed in the halls, he recognized the look in her eyes. She longed for a sign he would relent. There were moments when his resolve weakened, but she was not close when they occurred.

Alone, Art often chided himself for cloistered virtue. What would be his resolve if she were before him naked, if she insisted?

Strength came from his belief that knowledge of self, the expansion of consciousness he sought, would enable him to enter into a relationship impossible in his current state of existence. Until he achieved this higher level of being, any relationship, irrespective of its immediate gratifications, could not be whole and would lead to nothing, to inexorable emptiness.

In his own way, Carl tried to help. He sensed Art's ambivalence about Judith and took care that she and Keith Drumright worked together on the Freshman textbook committee. In a few weeks, Keith and Judith were lovers.

This union solved Keith's depression over Linda and the Russian wolfhound. From Carl's perspective, it kept temptation away from his friend. He told Art his pleasure over his solution to everyone's problems.

"I think I did a damn good job. You're no longer coveting your neighbor's wife, Keith's pimples are beginning to clear, and your old flame is getting what she wants."

His meddling irritated Art, but he knew the intentions were good.

"You're still an accessory to adultery," Art joked.

"What?" Carl asked puzzled.

"Keith and Judith, you put them together."

"I got her away from you as much as I could. What they decided to do is their business," Carl protested.

"Tell it to the judge."

Carl skipped to another subject. "Say, horse's ass, Linda, Rouge and I have narrowed our textbook choices. Tonight we're trying to decide which one to recommend. Do you have time to screen them and give us your pick?"

"I'll drop by the lounge for about half an hour. I promised Matt some moral support. He takes the qualifying exam Monday."

"Great, see you then."

That evening, Art thought he detected some sexual chemistry between Linda and Carl. He dismissed the idea, citing his own horniness as the culprit. After reviewing their choices, Art gave them his input, then left and drove to Matt's.

Virginia and Matt were in the middle of another skirmish in their ongoing war. He answered the door semi-intoxicated. She threw silverware and dishes around in the kitchen. Art indicated he could come back another time, but Matt insisted he stay.

"No, fuck her. Don't pay any attention to the bitch. She's on the rag. She's always on the rag."

As they seated themselves in the living room, Virginia emerged from the kitchen carrying a copy of *Psychology Today*. The cover depicted a woman bundled in a bale of cotton. The accompanying article was titled, "The Monthly Curse." She pushed the magazine under Art's nose and pointed at the picture.

"Yeah, there we are! Who gives a shit! Not you, not him. Don't pay any attention to her! That's his answer to everything. I'd like to see you two if you had to put up with this every month."

"Virginia, I'm sorry, but I had nothing to do with it and can't do anything about it," Art stated.

Matt leaped from his chair and grabbed the magazine. He turned from her and started to pull it apart. When she reached around him trying to reclaim it, his shoulder and elbow came up, solidly hitting her chin. Art caught her as her legs buckled, and gently slid her into the chair in which he'd been seated. Her eyes remained open, but glazed and crossed. Her mouth hung open.

"Jeez Matt, you coldcocked her!"

"Maybe now we'll have some peace and quiet," Matt said as he glanced at her. "She still won't shut her fucking mouth." He fell into his chair and started to roll joints.

Art grabbed some ice and a towel from the kitchen and held it to her chin. Her first signs of life were twitching movements, then her eyes started to clear and focus. When recognition returned, she grabbed the ice and towel from Art, leaped to her feet, ran into the bedroom and slammed the door behind her.

"Matt, I'm clearing out." Art rose and walked to the door.

"Man, don't leave. She'll settle down."

"I don't think so. You'd better talk to her," Art said as he left.

At the apartment, he read and waited for Carl. Art dropped off but was awaked at 2:00 A.M. by a telephone call from Rouge.

"Better get over to McGaw's right away. Big trouble."

"What happened?" Art asked.

"Virginia called us. Matt went nuts. She had to call the police. Darlene and I are going there now."

At Matt's apartment complex, police lights illuminated the night. Many of the neighbors stood around in bathrobes and pajamas. As Art approached the scene, he saw Fred the cat hanging from the upstairs railing, a belt around its neck. Virginia, crying, stood at the top of the stairs talking to two police officers, Red Dick and Darlene behind her.

Art followed the trail created by the police cars' flashing lights. Three Norman squad cars were parked on the near side of the complex. Matt, handcuffed, thrashed around in the back seat of one, shouting profanities and demanding his release. As Art approached the car, the officers leaning against it straightened up. "What can we do for you buddy?" one asked.

"He's a friend. Is there anything I can do?"

"Not now. He's spending the night with us."

"How bad is it?" Art asked.

"We got him for assault, cruelty to an animal, and resisting arrest."

"Can I talk to him?"

"He's too drunk. Wait till tomorrow. You might call a lawyer," one of the officers advised.

Art looked at Matt through the car window. Briefly, their eyes met, but Matt showed no trace of recognition. He continued to scream and kick the front seat of the car.

Art returned to the empty apartment. At some point, he dozed off in a kitchen chair. Carl's opening the door awakened him.

"What the hell are you doing up this early?" he asked.

"I haven't really been to bed. Where you been?"

Carl looked sheepish. "Got tied up."

"Great, Linda's into bondage," Art joked.

"No, man, it was just one of those things…"

"Just one of those fabulous flings, a trip to the moon on gossamer wings, just one…." Art sang.

"That's enough Dip Shit. I've got to tell you about this one." Laughing, Carl sat in one of the kitchen chairs.

"We went to her place to look at textbooks she used as a Freshman at

Oklahoma Baptist. We talked about our undergrad days, general BS. She twirled a baton at OBU. Showed me pictures of her in costume and told me how much fun she had twirling in front of the band. Next thing I know she runs into her bedroom and in about five minutes comes out dressed in her costume carrying a baton. She lives in an old Victorian house with high ceilings, and she actually started to twirl her baton for me. Talk about hysterical! There I am sitting on a sofa in her living room, and she's standing before me in this goofy costume throwing her baton twenty feet into the air. She's put on a few pounds and with her third toss, one of her boobs popped out of the costume. Without missing a beat, she stuck her boob back in, caught the baton and continued as though nothing had happened. Really bizarre."

Art laughed. "Sounds pretty Freudian to me, baton, naked breasts. Now you have to marry her."

"What are you talking about?"

"I told you what happened to me when I got involved with an Okie Baptist. Does Linda have to be saved now?"

Carl winced. "Let's forget it, okay."

"I will, but she won't." Art started to sing. "It was just one of those things..."

"Drop it!" Carl interrupted emphatically. "You never told me what happened with you."

Art related the evening's events, and Carl called Rouge. Virginia had spent the night there, upset but secure.

He hung up the telephone and turned to Art. "I can't believe he killed the cat."

"I know. He's been getting more and more crazy. He bitched about Fred the cat, but I never thought he'd do something nuts. When he punched her, I should have said something, at least stuck around."

"I doubt you could have helped. She hates you about as much as she hates him."

"In a couple hours, I'll call an old friend who's an attorney in town. We'll probably need some cash to get him out."

By noon, they had Matt out of jail. He wanted a beer, but Carl persuaded him to wait until they got back to his apartment. There, he proceeded to get shitfaced, screaming his hatred for Virginia and the English Department. They watched him until he passed out, put him to bed and left.

Monday morning, Art checked to assure Matt had regained consciousness and made it to the qualifying exam. At noon, he ran into him in front of the Student Union.

"What's going on? I thought the exam lasted all day," Art stated.

"It does, but I said fuck it. I completed about two thirds of the test, then left. I think I wrote enough to show them I know something about this English shit."

"You want to go for a brew?" Art asked.

"No, man, think I'll go home and crash. I'm still recovering from last week. Thanks again for getting me out of the shit house."

Back at the apartment, Art told Carl how Matt's actions and attitude puzzled him. Carl agreed.

"He's so screwed up on dope and booze, he doesn't know what he's doing."

"Are you going to say anything to him?" Art asked.

"I'll wait until he gets his exam results. They should be out before Brad and I get the word on ours."

"When will you hear something?"

"Nora said we should know by the second week in May. Those who made it have to go through orals." The telephone rang.

"Shit!" Carl exclaimed. "I know who that is. I'll take it in my room."

He emerged fifteen minutes later. "I'm going out for a while. If anyone calls, I'll be back in an hour."

"You want to talk about it?"

"Linda's been calling every hour. I've tried to put her off nicely, but it's not working. I'm going to meet her in the rare books section of the library and set this straight."

"You're going to MEAT her in the rare books section! I'm aghast! Have you no respect? And what are you going to say?"

"I'm going to tell her about Clare, explain what happened the other night was special, but can't be repeated," Carl stated with conviction.

"You mean it was just one of those things, just one of those fabulous flings, a trip to the moon on...."

Carl slammed the door before Art finished.

After two hours had passed, Art wondered if Carl and Linda had attempted to repeat the magic of the preceding night. The telephone's ringing interrupted his conjecture. It was Brad. "Carl asked me to call you."

"Where is he?"

"The University Dispensary," Brad answered.

"Dispensary? Is he all right?"

"I guess; meet me over there in about fifteen minutes."

He arrived before Brad and learned from the receptionist that Carl had been treated in Emergency with a head wound. He'd remain there for overnight observation. When Brad arrived, they went to see him.

One dim light above Carl's bed revealed his heavily bandaged head. His eyes closed, he appeared to be asleep. They stood on either side of the bed, trying not to disturb his rest.

"I'll bet they spent a fortune on bandages," Art whispered.

Brad laughed, and one of Carl's eyes opened. "Thanks for coming, Dipshits."

"What happened?" Brad asked.

"I met Linda in the rare books section of the library. She's writing some paper on the Bible as literature. I told her our night together was wonderful, but I had commitments. She pushed me on this, so I told her about Clare, that I planned to marry her. She cried, asked me to go over to her place one more time. If I could still walk away, we'd part with no hard feelings. I told her I couldn't; it wouldn't be fair to Clare. Then, calmly, she used both hands to pick up this huge book she'd been reading, turned away from me and with all the force of her body swung the book around and hit me squarely in the middle of my forehead.

"First I saw stars, then red, not anger, my blood. When the room stopped spinning, I was on the floor and medics were rushing me here. Turns out she clobbered me with a Gutenberg Bible."

Art doubled over laughing. Brad turned, trying to contain himself. "Where is she?" he asked.

"I don't know, but keep her away from me. I called you to see if your wife had any idea how bad this is."

"She said it's probably a mild concussion," Brad responded.

"That's what the doctor here said too."

"How do you feel?" Brad asked.

"My head's throbbing."

"Did you call the cops?" Art asked.

"I'm not going to press charges. She came here all weepy-eyed, begging forgiveness. I just asked her to leave. I'll need you guys to take my classes for a day or two. My head's splitting."

As Brad and he left the room, Art commented, "That's one tough way to get religion, but those Baptists are hell on converting the heathens."

Carl, eyes closed, responded by raising the middle finger of his ring hand.

When Nora interrupted Art in the middle of one of his lectures, he knew something serious had happened. "Your mother's on the phone. There's an emergency," Nora said.

A long distance call signaled a crisis. No matter what degree of financial security Art's mother attained, she could never rid her consciousness of the Great Depression she suffered through as a child. Using the telephone made no sense when a letter could accomplish the same end for a fraction of the cost. Other than a birthday card he sent to her in August, he hadn't communicated with her since his return to the States.

He dismissed his class and took the call in Eldka's vacant office.

"Hi, Mom?"

"Artie, is that you?"

The only name he hated more than Arthur was Artie. "Yes, what's wrong?"

"I had a terrible time getting hold of you. I'd lost your card, but I remembered you said something about teaching and going back to school. I called around and finally some nice man found your name and where you're at."

"Mom, what's wrong?"

"It's your grandfather, Artie, he died yesterday. We knew how close you were to him and thought you'd want to know."

He remained silent for a moment, absorbing the news. He hadn't talked to his grandfather, Degen, in years, but it hadn't lessened the love between them.

"Artie," his mother interrupted, "are you still there?"

"Yes, just thinking about Grandpa. What happened?"

"The heart thing again. He had another massive stroke. They tried to save him, but it wasn't no use. The funeral's in two days. If you can't come, it don't matter. We understand."

"No, I'll be there." He wrote down the relevant information and assured his mother he'd see her at the funeral parlor.

He called to find the timeliest and cheapest airfare and settled on a cattle run that took over four hours but got him into O'Hare at 8:00 A.M. the day of the funeral.

Alone in his office, Art read and re-read Thomas's "Do Not Go Gentle Into That Good Night." Intermittently, he reminisced about his Grandfather. The memories were a joy. A large man with a perpetual cigar in his mouth, Bernard Degen, or "Degen," as his friends and loved ones knew him, extended warmth and the joy of life to everyone he met. Unlike Art's father, Degen believed in a work ethic and labored diligently to make his small insurance business a success. Yet, he always found time to hold court at the neighborhood bar, telling stories and jokes and picking up more than his share of the tabs.

Degen believed in helping his friends, but his wife, Mother, made life miserable if she discovered it. They had little themselves, and she viewed his generosity as too dear to their family.

Art remembered sitting in Degen's lap on Sundays, listening to the Chicago Symphony. He loved Beethoven and Brahms and would tell Art stories about their childhoods in Germany, how their genius mirrored the underlying beauty and power of existence, somehow tapping into the godhead few could access. Bach, however, held the highest position in Degen's pantheon. Once he told Art: "Bach not only heard God's music, he shook God's hand." When the five-year-old exhibited skepticism, Degen looked knowingly at the child and nodded his head affirmatively. Art held his opinion in abeyance. Later, as a man, he agreed with Degen.

Although not handsome, his intelligence, knowledge and personality made Degen popular with the ladies. Art overheard his aunts' hushed stories about problems between their parents when the women were children. He made no judgment, deciding that if trouble existed, there were circumstances no one but the parties directly involved knew or understood.

Once, just before Art went into the service, he witnessed the charm his grandfather could still exert. Art, his mom, her husband, and Art's first love went to the North side to visit his grandparents. Degen had experienced his initial skirmish with the grim reaper, a stroke that had left his right side slightly paralyzed. Art had not seen him since before the trouble and was taken back at his appearance. He'd lost much weight, sat in a wheelchair hunched to the right side, and squeezed a rubber ball in his right hand. Art's concerns dissolved when Degen smiled. The light still glowed.

Art's young lady, at first hesitant about the situation, shook hands with Degen. He immediately offered her his ball. She declined, but Art noted the genuine smile that broke through her uncertainty. Within the hour, the girl, in Art's eyes the personification of beauty, sat in Degen's lap, laughing and joking. Before they left, she put her arms around his neck and kissed his cheeks and mouth. As Art said good-bye, amazement covering his face, Grandfather winked at him. When certain no one but Art could hear him, he said, "Come back later, I'll show you how it's done."

Ruth, Art's mom, was the second of five daughters and Degen's favorite. As a child, whenever Mother wasn't near, she'd curl into Degen's lap and talk him out of anything. If Mother arrived on the scene and learned Degen had surrendered the last of his change or allowed Ruth to listen to the new, obscene music, her leather strap came out, and she'd drive them both out of the house, screaming that their laziness and daydreaming would ruin them, the family and the country.

After Ruth married Art's father, a would be singer who spent his time between auditions reading comic books and beating her for making too little money, Degen's largess often kept Art and his younger brother from going hungry. Again, if Mother caught him slipping Ruth a few dollars, there would be hell to pay. But, in later years, Degen and Ruth became more sophisticated, and Mother's capture rate shrank. Usually, during the Sunday concerts in his grandfather's lap, Art fell asleep. When he awakened, Ruth stood there to pluck him up and take him home. Magically, in the little guy's pockets, dollar bills and change appeared. She'd collect this money as they walked home, enabling them to stop at the store and buy groceries. Ruth assured Art's silence by convincing him that if he told anyone, the good fairy who brought the money wouldn't come back.

The plane landed at O'Hare right on time. It took only twenty minutes by cab to get to the funeral parlor in the old neighborhood. With over an hour before the services started, he walked the streets he hadn't seen in almost thirteen years. Before his mother remarried and they moved to the South side, Art had zipped around every inch of these sidewalks on his tricycle. Distances he thought enormous were a few peddle-packed blocks.

He stopped at Degen's neighborhood bar. From the front steps he looked down the street to his grandparents' house. Cars lined the street. He knew his mom, her husband, brother, aunts, uncles and cousins were already there. He went into the bar.

After two double scotches, he asked the bartender if he knew Degen. The young man hadn't met or heard of him. Art reasoned incapacity had kept Degen from his old haunt for some years.

He looked around, amazed at the good business they did at 9:30 A.M. The faces had changed, but little else. He saw the same upright piano, wooden chairs and small tables. He could almost see Degen in the back, jacket off, tie mounted firmly to his multiple chins, cigar clamped firmly between his teeth, answering questions, discussing politics, drinking, joking, admiring the ladies. The laughter that came from deep within him permeated the bar's walls, but one had to have heard it to know it still existed there, silent, waiting for Degen or his ghost to pull it loose from the bar's inanimate objects. The young man tending bar had never heard it, nor had the mechanics, truck drivers or shift workers who'd stopped in for a quick bracer before going to work or home. What they had missed, what he missed.

Art grasped the importance of the moment, the need to live it thoroughly. It's all he had, all anyone has. Too late do people understand its importance, its transitory reality. "All is flux, savor the flux, do not grieve it on its way," he said to himself.

An hour later, he carefully climbed off the bar stool and walked back to the funeral parlor. His mother and brother greeted him at the door. She tried not to appear upset at his attire. He'd worn slacks and a decent shirt, but no tie. He'd borrowed one of Pollard's sports jackets. For him, this amounted to formal wear.

His brother, Ted, trying to make it as a pop singer, had flown in from Denver, where he had a job in a night spot. They hadn't spoken to one another in seven or eight years.

"You look prosperous," Ted stated.

"Thanks," Art responded, "You don't look bad yourself." He stared at Ted's five-hundred dollar suit. "Latest in lounge lizard this season?" Art asked.

Ted turned away without a response.

As expected, all his relatives were there. He wished he'd consumed more scotch. His grandmother, visibly shaken, seemed glad to see him. All the others harbored their private wars. Degen's two youngest daughters told Art how much pain Degen had endured the last week.

Ellen, the youngest, took pleasure in it.

"Seeing the way he treated Mother, it served him right. It was divine retribution." Her sister Edith, nodded her head in agreement. They looked at Art for corroboration. He glared at them, trying to keep his mouth shut.

When he didn't respond, Ellen continued. "I remember when we were little girls and that woman Papa had an affair with came to the house drunk and tried to get Degen to come out with her. She rang the doorbell, pounded on the door, swore like a sailor. It was terrible. Papa hid behind Mother, who had to get rid of her. The woman kept yelling 'Degen's got a good F___ left in him, Degen's got a good F___ left in him' over and over. Oh the neighbors! We were so ashamed. You don't know any of this, but the truth will win out," she stated with conviction.

"Do you know what it's like to be married to a shrew, a harpy?" Art asked.

Puzzled, both women shook their heads negatively.

"Listen to yourselves, look in a mirror, then ask your husbands who they're F___ing to find some solace in this bitch of a world," he said glaring at them, daring a response.

Ellen started, but decided better. They both whirled around and away. Now he didn't have to talk to them any more, and he'd probably taken care of their husbands and crazy children, a fair chunk of the gathering.

He went into the viewing room with the casket and sat away from the other mourners. When no people were viewing Degen, he went to visit him. Other than the usual pasty skin, he appeared almost alive. Art corrected one major omission by placing a cigar in Degen's upper suit coat pocket, assuring the tip could be seen.

"It's a good oneGrandpa, enjoy."

The tears burst forth, the sobs shaking his upper body, his anguish audible. Public displays were not his style, but he'd forgotten the presence of anyone but Degen and him.

A gentle hand brought him back. His Uncle Bob, Ellen's first husband, patted him soothingly.

"I'll miss him too," Bob said softly. Art dried his eyes on Pollard's jacket sleeves.

The man who had been Degen's pastor for almost forty years gave the eulogy. Half way through it, the pastor's tears started. They did not stop that day.

After the services, the procession of cars wound its way further north to the cemetery. Art sat with his brother and a few cousins in the third limousine behind the hearse. One cousin, an attractive, buxom young woman with helium between her ears, babbled about her first year at Southern Illinois University, where she'd managed a 1.5 grade average, the result of petty jealousies harbored by two flat-chested women professors who'd failed her. Art, numb, couldn't listen. Ted, intent upon seducing her, expressed outrage at the injustice she'd suffered.

At the cemetery, Art watched as Degen's pastor, in front of the casket, walked towards the grave and read from the Bible. Behind Degen walked his wife and their five daughters and their husbands. Behind them were their children with Art at the rear.

He marveled at the symbolism of the ritual, the procession, at its clear message of what they all faced. He thought about what they had to go through to get where they were, how they'd been shaped by forces over which they had little control, how they'd made do with what they had. To hate them for what they were or were not made no sense. They shared much heritage and had the fate of all humanity in common. Art experienced love and compassion for each of them. He felt the chains of anger break and free his body, his soul.

At the grave site, the family stood around the casket bidding Degen farewell, a few good riddance. Art, next to his mother, felt a sorrow he had not known existed, a heaviness that tugged at his insides, shrouded his soul.

In the midst of this grief, a surge of energy started deep within him. It began in the depth of his being, then rose through his entire body and transported some portion of him into the surrounding air. Miraculously, he saw everyone, including himself, from the spring sky. He experienced a serenity with which no prior euphoria could compare, all things united, all elements of existence at peace.

Art hovered above the scene, filled with the calm of knowing, the assurance that all was well, that an immutable order existed, one that they all shared. In this moment, he'd been graced with a glimpse of the harmony and ultimate oneness of existence.

For the second time that day, he cried, but these were easy tears of happiness elicited from the tranquil joy of his experience.

His mother's sharp slap on the arm brought him back to earth, literally.

"Stop your blubbering," she reprimanded.

Snapped back to reality, he could not be angry. He looked at the casket holding Degen's remains, then toward the sky and tacitly expressed his thanks for the experience, for the relief and hope it afforded.

After the funeral, the family went to Degen's favorite German restaurant. Art, sorting through his experience, could not eat. He wanted to talk with Degen's pastor about what had happened, but he did not appear. When the group started to break up, Art called a cab to drive him to O'Hare. His plane didn't depart until 5:30 A.M. the next morning, but he wanted to be alone. He manufactured his excuses, bid them his goodbyes, and left.

Awake all night in an airline terminal, Art thought about this day, a day on which he would build the remainder of his life. He'd been granted a brief glimpse of a reality he suspected existed, but one he hadn't expected to see until later in his spiritual maturation, if at all. He guessed that the shock of his grandfather's death, the personal loss, had transported him into this wondrous realm. The question remained how he could recapture and build upon this experience in the course of his day-to-day life.

Back in Norman, he called no one. For the remainder of the weekend and many days thereafter, he contemplated his brief, ecstatic trek into the miraculous.

CHAPTER SIXTEEN

Art watched in wonderment as the government accomplished with its troops what the Oklahoma radicals could not accomplish with their bomb. On May Day, 1970, U.S. Forces invaded Cambodia. Despite protestations from Washington, it appeared the Asian conflict had been expanded. Across the country, the students felt defeated; their outcry had failed to stop the war's escalation.

A crisis atmosphere engulfed the nation's campuses. Even Oklahoma University awakened. Most classes shut down the Friday of the invasion. Picket lines formed in front of every administrative and academic building.

Despite the energy and emotion surrounding him, Art did not allow his life to be disrupted and maintained his normal routine. In classes he taught, few students attended. Those who did wanted to discuss the invasion. He refused to be pulled into the debate and taught Yeats' poem, "A Prayer For My Daughter."

As each class ended, he reminded the students to check their syllabus for Monday's assignment and ignored the shock and disbelief registered in his students' faces. He knew that they had no idea of his inner turmoil, and he did not think it fair to them to voice his confusion.

Alone in his office, he sorted through the recent events in a context that made sense to him. It didn't seem useful to voice any opinion while he worked through myriad, often conflicting, thoughts and emotions. With this process, by maintaining control, he tried to promote order amid the potential chaos.

When he left campus early in the evening, the unrest had quieted. Students remained on the South oval discussing the invasion, but picket lines were gone and most anti-government chanting had stopped. Still, the atmosphere hung thick with dread, as though the concerns and anxiety expressed throughout the day had created a suffocating, exhausting layer of matter that permeated the air, making physical activity other than talk difficult, if not impossible.

In the apartment, he thought about Cambodia, Vietnam, and his experiences in that remote, yet ever-present part of the world.

Although he had started to understand the dynamics and problems of self that led him to Vietnam, he'd not come to terms with all events, actions he'd witnessed, actions in which he'd participated. With the immediate crisis, contemplation seemed a luxury. Everything had been accelerated.

His individual focus suggested a concept of duality, two Art Patowski's, then and now. The one in Southeast Asia, Mechanical Man, reacted to his environment like a machine or animal whose programming or innate reflexes result in prescribed responses to external stimuli. The person now, in Norman, struggled to become Organic Man, growing, understanding self as he evolves or is discovered, seeing his relationship to the animate and inanimate objects with which he interacts daily.

Organic man listens to an inner voice promoting harmony in tune with his essence. It goes beyond the force directing Mechanical Man, which leads him to embrace the status quo and the artificial.

The struggle between these two states of being continued, but awareness suggested growth: the completed versus the evolving, the static versus the organic.

From this dialectic, he intimated a third possibility: the future self, the individual who had achieved full consciousness, understanding and acceptance of his essence, the oneness suggested at Rainy Mountain and experienced at his Grandfather's funeral, the finite versus the infinite. This is the development he wanted, the state of being for which he must strive.

Nothing in this perception pardoned past activities, but it did offer the possibility of growth and a path for the future.

Saturday morning before Art left for the office, Matt telephoned. He'd received notification that he'd passed the qualifying examination at the M.A. level only. The English Department listed him as a Terminal M.A. He had to leave the university at the end of the current semester. Also in the mail was his notice to appear in court for his latest drunken rampage. Matt asked Art to join him later in the day for brew and commiseration.

He remembered Matt's reaction last semester to the results of the qualifying exam, but he could harm Fred the cat no more, and Virginia had moved out. Art told Matt he'd try to join him later in the day, but he couldn't commit.

In his office, Art labored with his play. He'd completed it a few weeks before and now rigorously edited with plans of sending it to a small troupe in Los Altos, California, who'd shown interest in producing it.

The campus had settled down from Friday's turmoil. The quiet enabled him to pursue his goal intensely, so focused that shadows from approaching night surprised him. He'd worked ten solid hours, completing the editing.

Sunday morning, he mailed the play to California. Close to 11:00 A.M., Matt called from the city jail. He'd been arrested Saturday night at O'Connell's Irish Pub for public drunkenness and resisting arrest.

Art arranged bail and drove him to his apartment. Matt invited him in, but Art declined.

"What's wrong, Man? You didn't come over last night, now you won't come in for a beer. You're not turning Puritan on me? You've been in the shithouse before."

"Matt, I don't give a damn if you spend all your waking hours in jail. That doesn't raise or lower you in my eyes, but I'm not going to bullshit. I'm having trouble with the cat thing."

"Killing that flea bag! Since when are you a cat lover?"

"What the hell does that have to do with anything? Why kill a living creature because you can't stand your wife or the English Department?"

"Well fuck you and the horse you rode in on!" Matt slammed the car door. "I'll send you your fucking money!" he yelled as he walked away. Art sat for a moment then left.

Monday morning, anti-war activities on campus increased. Without incident, Art and Carl crossed the picket line in front of Kaufmann. Neither said anything to their colleagues manning the lines or to each other. Each understood the other's ambivalence, but tacitly agreed that a sin of omission under volatile circumstances could prove less costly than a sin of commission, a view shared by many who have squeezed a trigger with another human being in the gun sight.

The sun shone brilliantly, but the early May breezes kept the temperature moderate. The promised super nova of spring had started, not in the sky but in flower beds, bushes, and trees around campus. These brilliant colors complemented the lush greenness of the grass and the pale softness of the blue sky.

Later that morning, on a campus not dissimilar from the one in Norman, bullets were fired, blood spilled. The unthinkable happened at Kent State.

Ohio National Guardsmen opened fired on unarmed campus protesters. Four students died.

Art had barely started a lecture when he heard the news from a student who arrived late to class.

"Yeah," he stated, "they don't know how many kids were killed. The National Guard went nuts and just started mowing 'em down."

Art, dazed, motioned towards the door. "Go, go on, no class today, class dismissed."

Talking excitedly, the students filed out of the room. Art sat motionless, the inside of his head spinning. When his equilibrium returned, he stared into his past, returning to the violence he'd witnessed and participated in, from the mean streets of South Chicago to those of Saigon and Ben Hoa.

"Now it's here," he thought aloud. "It's all here. I can't get away from it. No one can."

He rose, walked outside and joined the chanting throng, not caring where it marched. Quickly, noisily, the crowd found its way to the North Oval. On the Administration Building steps, a make-shift lectern had been erected. Mike Riter stood behind it, loudspeaker in hand. He cautioned restraint and reflection. A few students applauded his remarks, a few booed. The vast majority remained silent. Amazingly, Art perceived, "They're all listening."

Riter advised direct action, but counseled moderation. "We, unlike the people in Washington, can be heard without destroying those with whom we differ, those we would influence."

When Riter finished, the University's only black professor addressed the students and congratulated them on openly demonstrating their concerns. He talked about the war and its relationship to them and problems the country faced. Periodically, the crowd cheered his statements. Other faculty members, student leaders and a few university officials joined them to speak.

Art's mind raced through experiences related to the war and what had happened that day. He tried to connect all this to the ideas he'd been forming. His initial shock changed to resignation based upon his evolving understanding of the human condition. He felt disengaged from the situation and perceived Kent State and the issues associated with it in a broader sense, one that recognized that Vietnams, Kent States, all the injustices that existed globally would continue as long as humankind remained asleep, locked in its limited awareness of itself and its surroundings. He could do nothing about any of this. "All I can do is weed my own garden," he thought.

Art threaded his way through the crowd. When free of the mass, he felt the cool breeze bathe and refresh him, enforcing his feeling of liberation.

Carl and Brad were at the apartment when he arrived. "Mr. Cunning, to what do we owe this unsolicited visit?" Art asked.

"As I was telling Carl, this afternoon Manly asked me to attend a meeting tonight at his house. He's organizing some kind of political protest against the war. He wants a peace candidate to run against the incumbent U.S. Representative."

"Why'd he ask you?"

"He wants all the support he can get. Other faculty and grad students will be there. He asked me to invite you guys."

"What do you think?" Art addressed Carl.

"I don't know. I'm not ready to be classified a peace nix, but there are other considerations..."

"Like the general exams," Brad interjected.

"Aren't you the one who told me to go with what I thought was right and not worry about political ramifications?" Art asked Brad.

"Yes, and I still am. But who wants to trust his future to Manly and those other assholes?"

All three remained silent for a pregnant moment.

"I'm not going," Carl stated. "How about you two?"

"Since Manly invited me directly, I'll go to hear what they have to say," Brad answered.

"I'll join you," Art decided.

People from the University community and local denizens who opposed the war packed Manly's house. He expressed his plan to field a candidate who would run against the incumbent congressman in the July primary. The congressman's unqualified support of the war had rankled many of his constituents in Norman, the Cleveland County seat. Manly admitted, however, that beating him would be difficult, if not impossible. He'd been in office twenty-two years and was well liked and respected throughout his district.

"If we can't win," Manly recommended, "we need to find a candidate who can make a strong showing in the July primary. Are there any questions or comments?"

Art stood and addressed the group. "Why not have an Independent candidate waiting in the wings to pick up the organization after the primary loss. That way you'll have two shots at the incumbent and can keep the message in front of the voters through October."

Many in the group seemed to agree.

Manly looked uneasy. "I don't know where we'll get one candidate, more or less two."

"You have one right here," Brad started. "A scholar, war hero, who could ask for more!" He pointed to Art. Some people in the group applauded and voiced their agreement.

"No, No! I don't think so. Thank you all, though," he stated, wanting to kill Brad, who suppressed his laughter.

"Are you out of your mind?" he asked Brad under his breath as he sat down.

Before Brad could respond, Manly spoke. "Actually, we thought someone more in tune with the District's Democratic party would be appropriate. We have a couple of possibilities we'd like to discuss with the group."

Brad jumped to his feet. "Fine, use the one chosen for the Democratic primary, then let Art pick up the organization as an independent to make a run in November, keep the pressure on. We can't beat the system, but we can cause some pain." The group applauded the idea.

Manly addressed Art. "Are you over twenty-five?"

"I turned twenty-eight last March, but I'm not interested in running for political office."

"Do you have your Masters yet?" Manly asked.

"I finished it last semester," Art responded.

Manly seemed disappointed. "Well it's an idea."

"It's a great idea, war hero, young, energetic!" Brad continued.

Professor Candles, Art's Victorian poetry teacher from the past semester, stood. "I'm not certain it is such a good idea. Art isn't a native, and people around here tend to be somewhat xenophobic."

"Nonsense," Brad continued. "Look at him. He's your all-American boy. They'll never know how short he is, and we'll tell the public Patowski is an old Cherokee name that means noble soul, or some mumbo jumbo like that."

Many of the people laughed. Only Manly, Candles and Art looked unhappy. Before the meeting adjourned, all agreed that Manly would be responsible for finding a suitable Democratic candidate, and Art, despite his protests, would consider running as an Independent candidate.

At the apartment, Brad and Carl were laughing at Art's newly-found political existence. Art did not share their amusement.

"I'm not running for any political office, end of story. What got into you?" he asked Brad.

"The Independent candidate idea is yours, and somehow kissing babies, robbing the cradle, are linked in my mind with you. Seriously, you'd make a great candidate for all the reasons I mentioned."

"Bullshit! Start thinking about a way to get me out of this."

The next evening, Art did not attend the political meeting at Manly's house. Brad did, and continued to push the idea of Art's Independent candidacy. Manly, citing his absence, questioned Art's commitment.

Later that week, Manly and a number of his followers protested ROTC drills held at Owen Stadium. Waving an American flag, he led his group onto the field and occupied the south end zone until campus security forces removed them. The next day, his gait a bit more jaunty, he accepted congratulations from students and faculty. In the afternoon, he and Art crossed paths in Kaufmann.

"Where were you yesterday?" Manly asked accusingly. "I thought you opposed what we're doing in Southeast Asia."

"I do," Art responded, "but those kids you harassed didn't have a thing to do with the war. Some of them will be bleeding and dying soon so you can wrap yourself in a flag. Give them a break. Leave them alone."

Manly's mouth dropped open. "They need to be shown that responsible adults oppose what they're going into."

"Leave them to their choices. They can read, think and make up their own minds." Art abruptly turned and left.

The next day another late afternoon political meeting was scheduled. Art, on the agenda to discuss the viability of an Independent candidacy, had created a proposal. He planned to point out the reasons for having one and why he was not a good choice.

An hour before the meeting, he received an anonymous telephone call.

"If you show up for the meeting they're going to ask you about your affair with Judith Hunter and about some of your drinking habits. Tell your friend Cunning to mind his own business too."

"What! Who is this?" Art asked.

"I'm someone who doesn't want to see you hurt. I'm warning you, it won't be pretty," the caller hung up.

When Brad and Carl arrived, Art told them about the call.

"Jesus, what the hell is all this?" Brad asked.

"I don't know Sweat Lip, but you got me into a nice mess. I have to go tonight, but I don't want Judith brought into this."

"They won't say anything. It's a setup to get you to back out," Carl advised.

"I hope you're right. We'll soon find out."

Brad and Art arrived to a tense atmosphere. Obviously, some people hadn't expected him to attend. Manly went through actions items and assignments, then introduced their Democratic candidate, Keith Myers, a young attorney from Altus. A handsome, congenial man, Keith said a few words and fielded some questions. One person asked how he felt about an Independent candidate picking up his organization after the primary.

"I'm not certain we'll lose, but if we do, the Independent candidacy makes sense," Keith responded.

He asked if Art were there. He rose, shook hands with Keith and addressed the group.

"I think you've made a great choice, and I wish you all the luck in the world. If I'm here in July, I'll vote for Keith. I think you need to make the same kind of quality choice for your Independent candidate. I think the Independent idea is a good one because it will keep attention focused on the issue. View it as a continuation of Keith's attempt to educate people about the war. Winning's not the point. Morality is. The candidate's motto could be 'I can't lose, because I can't win.'

"One fact is clear, I'm not a quality choice for this task. I may not even be here this fall. You need a native Oklahoman who is willing to remain in the background until the time, if it arrives, is right. I'm not a politician, nor was meant to be, am an attendant lord, one that will do to swell a progress, start a scene or two, advise the candidate. No doubt an easy tool, deferential, glad to be of use, politic, to a point, cautious and meticulous. But not Prince Hamlet. No not at all." He paused, allowing a moment for recognition and laughter.

Scanning the audience, his demeanor changed.

"Before this meeting, I received a telephone call. The caller said allegations would be made if I came here tonight. Well, I'm here, and if anyone's going to make any allegations, please do it now." Art paused and looked out at the group. He noted those who lowered their eyes. After a full minute, no one responded.

"Good," he continued. "Whether or not the allegations were true has nothing to do with my decision to withdraw from consideration as your Independent candidate. I have to get on with my life, and I'm not the best choice. I wish you well, especially Keith. Whoever your Independent candidate is, I wish him well. All of you go forward in a noble and worthy cause; don't let partisan, topical concerns distract you from your goal. Thank you."

Art walked straight out of the house, with Brad close behind. Some of the people called Art, imploring him to stay. He never looked back.

CHAPTER SEVENTEEN

Manly's antiwar politics became the talk of the campus. Fliers inviting people to attend Keith Myers' campaign meetings appeared in sundry places, daily on the English Department bulletin board.

Art distanced himself from direct involvement, but kept his fingers on the pulse of Keith's efforts through a few English grad students who worked in the campaign. When Art asked about the Independent candidate idea, no one had heard further mention of it. He continued to wonder why anyone would want him out of the picture badly enough to threaten blackmail. His proposed candidacy seemed the only logical link.

Results of the Ph.D. General Exams diverted his attention from politics. Carl passed. Brad did not.

Ashen, Carl told Art his thoughts. "There's no way Cunning could have failed. I studied with the guy. He knew the material backward and forward, better than I did, better than any of the others."

"Could he have had a couple bad days?" Art asked.

"I doubt it. When we finished, he was the only one confident he'd done well. It doesn't make sense."

"What's his recourse?"

"None. He can't review the tests with his graders."

"You mean if Manly and Candles don't like the way Brad looks they can fail him with no fear of having to justify their grades?" Art asked.

"That's the system. I'm surprised you didn't know."

"I assumed you could learn what the problems were, especially if you want to retake the exams."

"He's free to talk to them, but they don't have to offer anything but general advice. Basically, there's nothing he can do. I'm going to Cunning's now. Why don't you join me?"

Brad's house resembled a wake, although the children helped everyone maintain perspective. Unaware of the blow their father had taken, the boys ran, fought and played as usual. Little Connell exercised her lungs and kept Marilyn busy. Her quiet strength reminded Art why Brad would be fine. The substance of their bond provided a refuge that no injustice could breach.

The three men walked outside to the back yard. "It's strange," Brad began, "I'm certain I passed. The tests were a piece of cake."

"You passed," Carl stated.

"Yeah?" Brad laughed. "Will you sign your Ph.D. over to me?"

"Are you taking them again?" Art asked.

"I doubt I could do any better."

"Something's really wrong," Carl added.

"I think it's that drop of sweat hanging off your lower lip. Do you think this bastion of culture wants a sweat king representing it?" Art quipped.

All laughed, but not much. Later, Art and Carl drove back to their apartment.

"I can't believe they did this to him," Carl commented in the car.

"But why?"

"I intend to find out," Carl stated emphatically.

That weekend Carl's Reserve group didn't meet. Friday night, Clare came in from Tulsa by bus. He picked her up in front of the Terminal Cafe and drove to the apartment.

"It's great to see you. I think your being here will help Marilyn," Carl commented in the car.

"How are they taking it?" Clare asked.

"Pretty well, but everyone's confused."

"Did Art have trouble finding a place to stay?" she asked as they entered the dark apartment.

"No, he's camping out with some kids he coached in little league. He looked forward to it," Carl replied.

Before she could find a light switch, he took her in his arms. "I've missed you."

"Me too," she responded. After a minute she pulled back from him. "I've been at work all day and on a bus over three hours. Give me a minute to clean up and get into something you'll like."

He held both her shoulders. The smell of her hair went straight from his nose to his groin. "Don't bother putting anything on."

While Carl looked for some appropriate music, Clare went into the bathroom with her night case, took off her dress, slip, and pulled back the shower curtain to run bath water.

"AHH!!!" Her scream pierced the night air, waking people throughout the apartment complex.

Carl crashed through the bathroom door. Eyes wide, she held her dress in front of her and pointed at the bathtub.

In the tub, wearing a rain coat, White Sox cap and catcher's mitt, Art squatted, drunk, pounding the mitt and yelling, "Put her right here baby, right here! Let me see what ya got!"

"What the hell are you doing!" Carl blared.

"Yummy," Art replied, never taking his eyes off of Clare.

Carl grabbed Art's raincoat, straightened him up and flung him over one shoulder. As Carl stormed out of the bathroom, Art's dangling head smashed into the door.

Outside, Carl hurled him onto the front lawn. You crazy bastard! Get out of here and don't come back!"

Art rolled over the lawn laughing. He sprung to his feet, squatted and pounded his fist into the catchers mitt, then ran into the night yelling, "Yummy, yummy!"

The next day, DeClines hosted a dinner for Clare. When Art arrived, only Matt hadn't shown.

"Where's your catcher's mitt?" Brad asked. "I hear the raincoat's going in the pervert hall of shame," DeClines commented. Everyone except Pollard and Rouge's wife laughed.

"Where's Clare?" Art asked Carl.

"In the kitchen, but she doesn't want to see you."

Art ignored him and went to her.

"Hi," he offered.

"Hello," she didn't turn around.

"You mad at me?" he asked.

"Don't come too close. I have a knife in my hand."

"I was just joking, trying to give everyone a laugh."

She turned to face him. "You scared me out of ten years. Carl said you'd really settled down the last couple of months. Then you do something crazy like that."

"I'm sorry. I didn't mean to upset you. After I'd gone through too much beer, it seemed like a funny idea, something everyone would enjoy."

What if I'd been naked?"

"Double yummy," Art responded as he raised an eyebrow and gave her his most impish grin.

"You're still crazy," she laughed.

Carl walked in. "Everything okay between you and the evil gnome?" he asked Clare.

Before she answered, Art asked, "Do you forgive me?" He tried to look humble and lovable.

"I forgive you," she opened her arms.

"I get a hug? I deserve one. Your big, ugly boy friend beat me up and threw me on the ground."

They embraced, and she patted his back.

Carl turned and grunted in disgust.

The evening went well. Food, wine, conversation and laughter flowed freely. No one mentioned academia. Art noticed each couple's closeness and basked in the friendship that permeated the gathering.

After dinner, they speculated how long Art had waited in the bathtub. Each person put up a dollar and guessed. Art gave the jackpot to the winner.

After he left, Art drove to Lake Thunderbird and slept under the stars. The spectacular sky and chirping crickets acted like a tranquilizer. Shooting stars illuminated the darkness, while crickets provided their close lullaby, reminding him of his place, his existence, somewhere between the angels above and the beasts below.

He didn't see Carl again until late Monday night. Art read in the living room when he arrived.

"Burning midnight oil for the oral exams?" Art asked.

"No, doing some detective work. It turns out two people graded Brad's Victorian exam. Four graded his American exam. One grader on the Victorian passed him; the other failed him. On the American exam, he received two passes, one low pass and a fail."

"How do those grades equate to failure?" Art asked.

"It's some fifty per cent rule that's not written anywhere, but they've used it forever. I also learned Manly and Candles gave him the failing grades, Davies the low pass."

"Four passes, two fails and he ends up with two failing grades. It doesn't make sense."

"What's more, Manly told two of his groupies he would get Cunning," Carl stated.

"Can we go to Eldka with that? Maybe he can do something."

"He can't do anything. You know how subjective all this stuff is. The guy who told me what Manly said is the same guy who called you before the meeting and told you they would expose your affair with Judith. I guessed right. They never figured you'd show."

"Who he is?" Art asked, surmising Nora had told Carl about the grades.

"I can't tell you. He told me with the promise of complete anonymity. He's an English grad student who'd be finished if this surfaced."

"What a screwing. But why all this intrigue?" Art asked.

"It's all politics," Carl responded. "Manly's been Chairman of the County's Democratic Party for years. Candles is his number two man. Both are locked into the Party. There's even talk about Manly running for elective office. The whole idea of a peace candidate is to control everything, make sure it doesn't get out of hand and hurt the Party as it has in other parts of the country."

"And for this, Brad's life gets turned upside down. Are you going to tell him?" Art asked.

"Yeah, when some time has passed."

"What horseshit! That does it for me. I'm getting out of here after this semester."

"This is sudden," Carl responded, taken back.

"I've been thinking about leaving for the past couple of months. I'm not sure where I'll go, but I need to get away from all this bullshit, do something different. I'm getting close to thirty and still don't have anything practical I can do for a living."

"You can always make a living."

"True, but I need to live. I don't think I'm doing that here. Better start looking for a new roomie."

"When will you leave?"

"I'll stay here or at least pay my share of the bills through next month. If someone wants to move in before the end of June, I'll move on. I have a general idea where I want to go, probably the West Coast."

"You think it'll be better there?" Carl asked.

"It'll be different. I need a change."

"I'm surprised, but understand."

"For scheduling purposes," Art asked, "when do your oral exams start?"

"Next week. Two days in front of the inquisition."

"You'll survive, though it won't be fun. Last semester, Davies told me he relished them, delighted in being an asshole, said it gave him his last shot at the people."

"Thanks. That makes me feel better."

Art smiled. "You'll do well. Just don't let them keep you from laughing."

"That may be tougher than it sounds."

That evening, Art stayed awake thinking about his decision to leave. He hadn't made up his mind until Carl told him Cunning's situation. That sealed it, brought everything to the proverbial head. Uncertain of his destination, the lure of the West Coast beckoned. He liked the idea of trading red clay for sand and surf, the dreary Oklahoma flatness for the rolling mountains and lush valleys of the Bay Area. A new idea for a play had started to churn in his mind's eye, assuring spiritual nourishment, and he'd saved enough money to subsist while he searched for a job.

The only difficult part about leaving was Judith. The thought of not being close to her brought a strange mixture of pain and pleasure. Art missed her terribly, but he could not forget his pledge or the pain their relationship had caused.

Carl's orals went as Art had anticipated. Davies gave him a bad time, but Eldka's unexpected presence kept him calmed down. The professors addressed more questions to each other than to Carl, continuing arguments that had gone on for years. After the second full day, they asked him to wait outside the room while the panel decided his fate. After twenty minutes, they called him back and extended their congratulations to him on passing. He tried to appear happy and gracious, but Brad's situation remained centered in his mind.

Upon extricating himself, he went to Art's office. "I hoped you'd be here."

"How'd it go?" Art asked.

"Wonderful, if you enjoy arguing about how many angels can dance on the head of a pin. I passed."

"Congratulations," Art rose to shake his hand.

Carl didn't respond. "I don't take any pleasure from this."

"Because of Cunning? There's nothing you can do about it. Remember, you told me."

"It's so rotten."

"Write your dissertation as quickly as possible and get the hell out of here," Art advised.

"My exact plan. I can't think of any other option."

Carl paused for a moment. "Memorial Day weekend is coming up. I'm going to Tulsa and wondered if you'd like to join me. Clare can probably fix you up with one of her friends."

"Thanks, but I need to stay here and get ready for finals. They start next Thursday."

"Are you okay? You've been living like a monk."

"Yeah, Rasputin."

"Seriously, other than the bathtub incident, which I think I understand, you haven't been your usual gnomic self."

"I'm fine, just have a lot to think through."

"If you change your mind, let me know."

Carl left, but his sorrow lingered after him, the inequity committed against Brad compounded by Carl's inability to enjoy his success.

Art's thoughts were interrupted by a knock at his door. Judith stood there, beautiful, tentative. He hadn't seen her in over four weeks. It seemed longer. Electricity coursed through his body, the physical heat she awakened.

"May I come in?"

He stood, unable to disguise his pleasure. "Of course." As she sat, he closed the office door. "This is like old times," he said softly.

He went to her and lifted her face to his. She responded, but he pressed down on top of her shoulders, not allowing her to rise.

"God, I've missed you," he murmured, stroking her face with both his hands, marveling at the juxtaposition of colors, the blue eyes, black hair, red lips, the porcelain whiteness of her skin. "She could have been a song that Homer sung," he uttered aloud, wiping away tears that blossomed at the corners of her eyes.

"Don Juan was almost saved from hell by one heart felt tear of genuine love," Art commented.

He sat before all his resolve vanished, but took one of her hands and held it on the desk with his. "What a great surprise. Does Keith know you're here?"

"That ended two weeks ago. I moved into an apartment about the same time. Larry and I split up."

"Because of Keith?"

"Because of everything."

"What happened with Keith?"

"At best, we were a convenience to each other. He wanted Linda. I wanted you. After what we had, I always felt dissatisfied."

He stood and had her rise. After they kissed, he removed her sweater and reacquainted himself with her breasts. When he removed her jeans, she begged him to take her.

"Please hurry," she pleaded. "I missed you so."

"I have to taste you," he gasped, carefully placing her on his desk and spreading her thighs. He licked, sucked and probed until her groans rose to roars and his penis strained for relief. He entered her luscious juiciness, experiencing a moment of release at being inside of her followed by an increased intensity that continued until his throbbing climax sent shudders through his entire body, and he almost fell to the office floor. She followed, not bothering to suppress her screams of delight.

They laughed at their noise.

"I don't hear the janitor or police," he joked. They made love for hours, on the floor, standing, kneeling, in his chair, back on the desk. When finished, he sat naked, sated, exhausted. She lounged on the floor between his legs, stroking and kissing his limp penis, thighs and legs. He ran his hand through her hair and over her shoulders and back. Slowly, they helped each other dress.

Outside, the late May weather remained moderate. A spring breeze had just enough strength to make its presence known. They held hands. Nothing really right, yet everything fine because they were together.

On campus corner, Jim and Wendy sat glassy-eyed with their German Shepherd, radio blaring. The couples waved to each other. Jim then made a peace sign and yelled for everyone within earshot to hear, "To ball is to live; all else is waiting!"

Inside Orin's, Art ordered a pitcher of beer. He thought of being there with Melanie, then with Lauren when they ran into her. He thought of all that had happened in one year.

"Judith, much has happened over the past year. Christ, over the last six months! I've been thinking about what I want to do, where I want to go. I've decided to leave after this semester."

"Where are you going?" she asked, voice hushed, eyes lowered.

"I'm not sure, maybe the West Coast."

"You're not going to finish your Ph.D.?"

"Probably not, certainly not here."

"What brought this on?"

"I've started to make up my mind about some things, about myself. To continue the process, I need to get out of here, go some place new. There's an institutional corruption here that's as rotten as anything I saw in the military."

"You can't run away from it," she argued.

"I'm not running away. I'm going to something."

They said little more. He walked with her to her new apartment, only a few blocks away.

"Do you want to come in?" she asked.

"Not tonight. If you don't have plans for the weekend, I'd like to see you."

She looked at him wistfully. "I'd like that."

"Good, keep Saturday and Sunday open." They kissed good night, and she smiled at him as she closed the door.

That weekend they picnicked at Lake Thunderbird, remembering and laughing about their first meeting.

"Whatever happened to that girl?" she asked.

"Last I heard, she's still in Norman. I haven't seen her for a while." He held Judith close. "Want to go over to the tall grass?" he joked.

"It's too cold."

"That's what she said."

They laughed, talked, and played in the water. As they shared a bottle of wine, he read from his play and discussed his idea for a new one. With the last light of day, they held each other and watched the spring sun disappear.

The rest of the weekend, in his apartment, they devoured each other, food and a baggie of grass she'd brought.

Late Monday, he drove to her place. "Will I see you before you leave?" she asked.

"Definitely. I'll be here all or most of June. I told Carl if he found a new roomie before I left, I'd get out or move on."

"If you're not ready to go, you can stay with me," she offered.

"I might never leave."

"That would be fine," she said as she snuggled next to him in the car.

Finals started four days into June. Art took both of his on the same day. He didn't administer any exams until the following Monday.

Carl had Brad, Red Dick and Art meet him at the Terminal Cafe with their Masters Degrees. He took pictures of them under the Terminal Cafe sign, holding their terminal MAs in front of them. He'd invited Matt, but he chose not to attend. Matt had not yet received his diploma and didn't think the idea funny.

When finals were finished, Carl had to rush off to Marine summer camp. He asked Art to screen all roommate applications.

Carl would not return till mid July and wanted Art to stay until then, using Carl's room if he signed up a new roomie. Intuitively, Art declined, anticipating the need to leave early.

Before going their separate ways, Carl arranged an end of academic year good-bye dinner at Cunning's house. Clare came in from Tulsa. (She checked the bathtub before undressing.) Rouge showed up alone. Matt, again, refused the invitation. Each felt genuine sadness at this parting of the ways, but all had been there before and, essentially, all but Art remained intact.

Art knew how much he would miss them. Each person embodied aspects of strength and wisdom that would be manifested in their lives, and in the lives of their children and their children yet to be born. He also recognized that his spiritual journey would be different from theirs, not better or worse, but different.

As he left, Brad's wife, Marilyn, hugged him. Clare kissed him on both cheeks. "You be a good gnome now," she drawled in her best Texas accent.

"Just remember," he replied, "there's more to life than living with a moose in a lean-to in New Mexico. Soon, I'll have a tree house in California. You're always welcome."

Carl held out his hand. "I don't know if there's anything to what Cayce writes, but we'll meet again, I'm certain."

Art nodded. "I think our paths crossed before."

Brad extended his hand. "Good luck, Traveler."

"You too wretch. Take care of that great family."

Art shook hands with Rouge, closed his eyes and began to snore.

In the middle of June, Art's happiness soared when he received a letter from the drama troupe in California. They wanted to perform his play and asked him to join them to discuss production and casting. They planned to start rehearsals in August and performances by late September.

With the money he'd saved over the past semester he could afford to go. He sent a signed copy of the contract to the troupe and told them he'd be out there after the July 4th weekend. He tuned his VW and invested in a new set of tires.

His departure tempered Judith's excitement about the play, but they celebrated quietly, holding one another and drinking champagne under an incredible late spring sky. Venus, Mars, and Jupiter formed a perfect isosceles triangle, with Venus and Mars at the base, parallel, and Jupiter at the apex, looking down on them. Venus's brilliance illuminated the evening sky, enhancing Mars' deep red glow. Art had never seen them so close.

Without taking his eyes off of the brilliant show, Art addressed Judith: "Some scientists say that the universe is finite, that it's contracting, caving-in on itself. What if everything, time, space, matter, goes back to that single kernel of energy, and the big bang happens over and over again and again and again? We keep doing it until we get it right or God just gets sick and tired of the whole thing and stops it forever."

"We've been here before. You feel it, and so do I. How could we remember anyone or anything?" Judith asked.

"Once out of time, there is no time. A billion years, two trillion years, none of it means anything. But while we're here, we have to work at making it right, whatever right is."

Packing did not take long. His books, the major part of his belongings, were already boxed from cleaning out his office. He went by the Department and said farewell to Eldka, Pitts and Nora. Eldka told him he'd be welcomed back if he changed his mind. Pitts bent an elbow with him and thanked him for his work on the Freshman textbook committee. Nora, unable to disguise her concern, asked Art if he thought Carl were safe. He assured her Carl would return soon and, as long as he stayed out of the woods, he'd be fine.

The next morning, unannounced, he went to Matt's apartment. When Matt opened the door, his face burst into a grin.

"How the hell are you, Man! Come on in!" He opened two beers. The apartment was in shambles.

"This place looks almost as good as Gary's," Art laughed.

"Yeah, Garnett's my interior decorator. I'm going to have the walls done in Boris Karloff and Bela Lagosi characters," Matt rejoined.

"How is that crazy bastard?"

"I don't know," Matt answered. "I haven't seen him in a month. He's generally one step ahead of the law. What have you been up to?"

Art told him about his decision to leave and what had happened with the play. Matt expressed his excitement.

"Great, the next Eugene O'Neil, right here. I can tell people how we spent the year shitfaced together."

"What are you doing?" Art asked.

"Looking for a job. I went on four interviews in Oklahoma City this week."

"What kind of work?"

"Anything. I decided to stay here a year, save some money before I head back to Colorado. Speaking of, the mail should be here. Let me check."

Matt returned in a minute. There were no job responses, but he'd received a large envelope from the University containing his Masters degree. He went to his bedroom and returned with a full lid of marijuana, sat in the chair next to Art, and poured the marijuana on top of the degree. With Art's assistance, he rolled the degree, using scotch tape to hold it together. He twisted both ends closed, leaving a small gap for inhaling in one.

While Art laughed, Matt lit the giant joint and inhaled, lit it again and offered it to Art. It took a few hours and a couple of six packs, but, eventually, they smoked Matt's Masters degree.

The next day, lying in bed trying to recover, the local paper shocked Art out of his hangover. On the back page of the *Norman Transcript* he read Lauren's fate: "The coroner's autopsy proved conclusively that the death of Lauren Longley, 20, from Purcell, was caused by a substance over-dose."

Shock reverberated though his body. The remaining information in the article indicated they'd found her three days before in her apartment on East Boyd Street. There were no signs of foul play.

At the Norman Police Department, because Art wasn't a family member, the uniformed officer refused to speak to him. His persistence earned him a brief meeting with the detective who handled the case.

"I understand you were her teacher," he started. "Sad case, beautiful young girl like that. You can imagine how her family's taking it."

"Can you tell me what happened?" Art asked.

"Looks pretty straightforward, she overdosed. The only question is did she do it on purpose? There were no notes or anything, but judging from the amount she took, I'd guess she knew what she was doing."

"You mean suicide?"

"That's my guess, but I'll never prove it. Besides, what's the point? Her family has enough grief. I'd like to get my hands on the prick who sold the shit to her."

Back at his place, Art retrieved Lauren's X-rated movie. He'd planned to throw it into the Canadian River as he left town. He drove to a photography store in Oklahoma City and swapped out the film's media. The next day he called Barry Trevor, a young man he'd coached in Norman little league nine years before. Barry now worked as a reporter for the *Norman Transcript* and agreed to meet Art at Dinko's, a greasy spoon on Main Street.

Barry, a tall, gangling young man, smiled when he saw Art.

"Mr. Patowski, how are ya? It's been a long time."

"Good to see you, Barry. How are you and your family?"

"Fine, thanks. I read what you did at the Armory a couple of months ago. It was great. I bragged to all my co-workers about my former little league coach. It was a surprise to hear from you."

"What I called about isn't pleasant. As a reporter, you agree to protect your sources, right?"

"You bet!" Barry responded.

"The girl who overdosed a few days ago, Lauren Longley, was my student last fall. A while back I saw this." Art patted the bag containing the film. "It's a porno flick. She's in it. I confronted her and asked what was going on. She told me she'd gotten into drugs, started making money from the films to pay for her drugs. I offered to help, but she made me promise to stay out of it, said she was happy and not doing anyone any harm. Right or wrong, I agreed. One of her professors is in the film and helped produce it. From what she said, he might have had something to do with her supply of dope too."

"What's his name?" Barry asked as he wrote hurriedly in a tablet.

Art told him and explained what little else he knew.

"I'm sorry I didn't speak up earlier. But I promised her I'd mind my own business. Then I saw the article in the paper. Can you be certain I won't be connected with this?"

"Sure, the film's from an anonymous source. I received it in a plain brown bag. What a story! An OU philosophy professor lures coed into drugs and pornography."

"Before you get too carried away, remember, she has a family. Think of them. This should be handled discreetly."

Barry took a deep breath. "I hear you. I got too excited. I know some people on the Norman Police Force. They'll handle it carefully. The University and the city don't need this kind of publicity."

After the meeting, Art drove to Max Hanna's house. Max opened the door only because he was too stoned to recognize Art.

"Who are you?" Max asked.

"Lauren's old English teacher, asshole!"

Art was inside the house before Max could slam the door shut.

"What do you want?" Max yelled, taken back by Art's physical entry.

Art told Max what he knew and what he'd done with the tape.

"What makes you think anyone can prove anything?" Max yelled.

"Dumb shit! They have pictures of you fucking your students. Figure it out!"

"Why are you telling me this?"

Art paused. "To give you a chance to get out of town so her family doesn't have any more pain. I also have this for you." Art's right cross came from the depth of his being and landed squarely on Max's jaw. He fell backwards into a corner and was halfway up when Art's solid right hook put him down again. A trickle of blood appeared from the left side of Max's mouth. He raised his right arm but did not turn his face upwards to Art.

"Don't hit me again," Max cried.

Art overcame his urge to kick Max's head in and backed away. "Get out of here and get out fast!" Art warned as he stormed out of the house.

Judith shared Art's last night in Norman. She held him as though her embrace could prevent his departure, as though her failure to sleep could stop the new day's arrival. In the early morning, her crying awakened him. He put his arm around her and gently placed her head on his chest.

"It's all right," he murmured.

"Can I go with you?" she asked.

"It's not the right time," he answered.

"Will it ever be?"

"I don't know. It's difficult for me to conceive of wanting anyone more than I want you."

"Why leave, or why not take me with you? What are you looking for?" she asked.

"Myself, my essence, what I really am, stripped of all the baggage. If I find out who I am, I can be of worth to you and myself."

"It's my lying to you, that's why you won't take me," she cried.

"We lied to each other. What's happened to us, our past, isn't important except as it relates to right now. What's tough is figuring out the relationship of things. How, through all the events and circumstances, the past connects to a specific moment. For the most part, it seems impossible. But that's part of what I'm trying to do, and I need the objectivity another place will give me."

"Then you've forgiven me."

"Of course, but all debts are due and owing. They must be paid, yours and mine."

"I don't understand," she pulled away from him.

"The ultimate importance is living one's life in the moment, assuring no new debts are created. Neither you nor I are capable of doing that. If we stay together, the end is predictable, and it isn't nice," he stated with conviction.

She stood and paced, her exasperation visible. "What do you want to do with your life? I know it's something beyond writing plays and making love to me. But I don't know what you're talking about. It's abstract crap!"

"I hope not, but I'm not sure I understand everything I'm thinking either. Life is a series of small funerals preparing us for the big one, our own; but something happened to me at my grandfather's funeral, something special. I know there's more out there I have to look for. If I find it, achieve the understanding I'm after, I may be able to write something of value, through my plays forge some portion of the path from this world to a greater state of consciousness. Now, I can't do it."

"Why don't you take a consciousness-raising class, for God sake!" she exclaimed.

"Why are you so put off with me?" he asked.

"I want to provide you with what you're looking for, but I don't understand a word you're saying!" she responded.

"What I'm seeking is not what they're talking about in consciousness-raising classes. It's linked to the ultimate source of human potential in the sense of the perfect representation of Idea, the manifestation of the essence of concept."

He stood and took her in his arms. "I can't take you there. I'm not certain I can get there."

She stayed awake the rest of the evening, looking at him and running her hands over his body, attempting through her senses to take a portion of his being into hers and to possess him with a part of her for eternity. He sensed her vigil as he occupied a cloudy realm between sleep and consciousness.

He dreamed of a lush forest where he and an unknown lady frolicked like children, following a bearded man who led them to a huge tree with an opening at its base. The man motioned for them to join him in the tree, but both were hesitant. Upon taking his first step to join the man, Art awakened.

In the morning, Judith and Art parted with few words. He managed his pain by thinking of the future and its possibilities.

Because his VW had no air conditioning, he had planned his driving for late afternoon, evening and early morning hours, sleeping through the afternoon's heat in the cool comfort of motels.

Early in the evening, his stuffed VW limped down Lindsay Street to Interstate 35. An unexpected breeze pushed at his back, helping him on his way. At the crossroads, he took one last glance back. From that moment on, he looked towards the sun.

The End